The Cafe Cook Book

The Cafe Cook Book

Italian Recipes from London's River Cafe

Rose Gray and Ruth Rogers

Broadway Books   New York

Food Photography **Martyn Thompson**   Black and white Photography **Jean Pigozzi** Design **the Senate**

In the summer of 1994 the River Cafe was redesigned to create a larger, more exciting space, with an Italian wood-burning oven as its focus. Just as we were inspired by the char-grill ten years ago, we are now passionate about the oven's immediacy and responsiveness. It has opened up all kinds of opportunities for doing what we enjoy most – mixing the traditional with the modern.

We discovered how roasting at a high temperature intensifies the flavor of dishes such as porcini stuffed with pancetta and thyme. Roasting slowly, as the oven cools down, also has very special results – a shoulder of pork, for example, rubbed with fennel seeds, garlic and chile achieves a succulent flavor reminiscent of *porchetta*, traditionally sold from vans and market stalls all over Tuscany. We wrap artichokes with thyme in foil, squash ripe plums and apricots on vanilla-scented bruschetta, stuff pheasants with ricotta and sage and cook them all in the wood oven.

Experimenting at home with our domestic ovens, we achieved the same delicious effects by roasting at a high temperature on the low rack of the oven. Equally, by slow roasting, and ideally using an oven brick to increase the moisture, you can roast overnight very successfully. All the recipes titled 'wood-roasted' use these techniques.

The Cafe Cook Book begins with seasonal fruit drinks as they begin the meals we serve in the restaurant. They range from freshly squeezed white peaches and sparkling dry Prosecco, an exuberant summer special, to freshly squeezed pomegranate mixed with Campari and Prosecco, a delicious winter aperitivo with a beautiful color.

Our second chapter, 'antipasti' in a traditional Italian meal, includes many of our favorite, simple starters – hardly recipes, just the pulling together of the finest ingredients to achieve classic dishes such as prosciutto with crisp Savoy cabbage, sweet aged balsamic vinegar, and Parmesan, or a simple summer vegetarian carpaccio – slices of young zucchini marinated in lemon juice and extra virgin olive oil with shavings of Parmesan and arugula. These recipes and others reflect our open approach to planning a meal, with many dishes that can be eaten as part of a meal or work equally well on their own.

Fish has increasingly become a focus of our main courses, reflecting a change in our customers' preference. We have discovered and adapted many regional Italian recipes such as a variation on inzimino from Umbria, using salt cod, and baked whole loin of tuna with coriander from Sicily.

We have found new ways to cook duck, venison, and game, changing traditional recipes to include other meats, for instance bollito misto with duck. Butchers have responded to our need to know about the breeds and feeds of animals and we love to cook the wonderful organic pork which is becoming increasingly available.

On recent trips to Italy we visited the wine and olive estates at Felsina and Selvapiana to select olive oil. We also went to the regions of Puglia and Sicily, where talking to cooks and producers we learned about their vegetables – cima di rape, ceci, and cicoria – spices, and the semolina bread called pagnotta.

The recipes in this, our second cookbook, have been stimulated by all these experiences and reflect the food we love to cook and eat at The River Cafe.

Rose Gray & **Ruth Rogers**
The River Cafe, London, 1997

Dri

nks

1

Moscato d'asti con cedro fresco
Moscato d'asti with fresh lime

For 6-8 This is a winter drink. You need to use a cocktail shaker with a perforated top.

6-8 limes, fridge cold
1 bottle Moscato d'Asti, cold

Squeeze the juice from 5 of the limes. Slice the sixth.

Pour the lime juice into the shaker. Add the Moscato very slowly, stirring gently, as it will immediately fizz up. Cover with the perforated top – this will stop the fizzing – and pour gently into champagne glasses. Serve with a slice of lime.

Spumante con borragine
Spumante secco with borage

For 6-8

2/3 cup superfine sugar
1 cup water
10-15 fresh borage leaves, washed
juice of 2 lemons
1 bottle Spumante Secco or Prosecco,
    fridge cold
at least 12-16 borage flowers

Using a small heavy-bottomed saucepan, dissolve the sugar in the water, heating gently to make a syrup. When the syrup is hot, add the borage leaves. Stir and allow the borage to just wilt in the syrup. Remove from the heat, and cool. Strain the syrup, then add the lemon juice.

Put the syrup in a pitcher or cocktail shaker, add the wine (two-thirds wine to one-third syrup), and stir. Pour into champagne glasses, adding a few borage flowers to each glass.

Bellini I

For 6-8

8 ripe yellow peaches
1/2 cup superfine sugar
a good shot of Vecchio Romagna (Italian
    brandy)
1 bottle Prosecco, fridge cold

Preheat oven to 400° F.

Halve the peaches and remove the pits.
Place the half peaches in an oven-proof
baking dish and sprinkle with the sugar
and Vecchio Romagna. Cover with foil
and seal. Bake the peaches for 15-20
minutes. They should become slightly
softer and the juices will begin to run.
Remove from the oven and allow to
cool.

Put the peaches and their juices in a
food processor and pulse-chop. Push
the pulp through a fine sieve.

Using a large cocktail shaker or pitcher
with a lid, pour in 4 champagne
glassfuls of peach purée, and add the
same volume of Prosecco. Stir with a
long spoon to combine and also to
prevent over-fizz. Pour into champagne
glasses through the lid of the cocktail
shaker.

Bellini II

For 6-8

10-12 ripe white peaches
1 bottle Prosecco, fridge cold

Choose very ripe white peaches. Cut
them in half and remove the pits. Using
an orange juicer or reamer, press the
juice from the peaches as you would
from oranges.

Pour the peach juice into a pitcher or
cocktail shaker with a lid. Add the same
volume of Prosecco and stir to control
the fizz and consequent overflow. Cover
with the lid, and pour gently into
champagne glasses.

Arance sanguigne e prosecco
Blood oranges and prosecco

For 6-8

8-9 blood oranges, according to juice
    obtained
1 bottle non-vintage Prosecco

Squeeze the oranges into a cocktail shaker or pitcher. Add a little Prosecco and stir with a spoon to still the fizz, then add about two-thirds of the remaining wine (you want to have slightly less orange juice than Prosecco). Pour into champagne glasses through the perforated top of the cocktail shaker.

Melone e prosecco
Melon and prosecco

For 6-8

1 very ripe cantaloupe
juice of 1 lemon, or 1 1/2 limes
1 tablespoon superfine sugar, or more
1 bottle Prosecco, fridge cold

Cut the melon in half. Scoop out the seeds and put them in a fine sieve over a bowl to collect the juices. Scoop the rest of the ripe pulp from the skin and put in a food processor. Pulse-chop to liquefy. Sieve the pulp, adding it to the melon juices collected.

Add the lemon juice and 1 tablespoon sugar to the pulp. Add more or less sugar according to the sweetness of the melon.

Use a cocktail shaker or pitcher to mix the drink. Fill to slightly over half full with the melon juice. Add enough Prosecco to come to the top. Mix to combine and pour into champagne glasses through the perforated top of the shaker to contain excess fizz.

Fragole e prosecco
Strawberries and prosecco

For 6-8

18 ounces very ripe strawberries
juice of 1 1/2 lemons
3 tablespoons superfine sugar
1 bottle Prosecco, fridge cold

Remove the hulls from the strawberries. If muddy, wash carefully, and lay out on a cloth to dry. Make sure the fruits are very dry.

Cut the strawberries in half and put in a food processor with the lemon juice and sugar. Pulse-chop to a liquid pulp. Strain the pulp through a fine sieve.

Mix in a cocktail shaker equal parts of strawberry and Prosecco. Pour into champagne glasses using the perforated top of the shaker, as the drink will otherwise fizz up and over.

Lamponi e prosecco
Raspberries and prosecco

For 6-8

18 ounces ripe and sweet raspberries
1/2-2/3 cup superfine sugar
1 bottle Prosecco, fridge cold

Wash the raspberries and shake dry. Put in a food processor with the sugar, and pulse to a liquid. Push the pulp through a fine sieve.

Mix the pulp with the Prosecco in a large pitcher or cocktail shaker. Stir to calm the fizz and pour slowly into champagne glasses, using the lid to prevent overflow.

Ribes nero e prosecco
Black currants and prosecco

For 6-8

9 ounces fresh black currants, stems
    removed
2/3 cup superfine sugar
1 bottle Prosecco, fridge cold

Wash the black currants, and put in a saucepan with the sugar. Gently heat to allow the fruit to burst and release their juices. Do not boil. Remove from the heat and cool quickly. Push the pulp through a fine sieve.

Make sure the purée is completely cold, then mix with the Prosecco in a large pitcher or cocktail shaker. Stir to combine, then pour into champagne glasses. Use the lid to contain the fizz and prevent overflow as you pour.

More e prosecco
Blackberries and prosecco

For 6-8

1 1/2 pints ripe blackberries
1/2 cup superfine sugar
1 bottle Prosecco, fridge cold

Put the blackberries and sugar in a food processor and pulse-chop to a purée. Push the purée through a fine sieve. Test for sweetness, as blackberries can be sour. Add more sugar if necessary.

Mix the purée in a pitcher or cocktail shaker with the cold Prosecco and pour into champagne glasses through the lid or top of the shaker to contain the fizz.

Pompelmo rosa e prosecco
Pink grapefruit and prosecco

For 6-8

3 pink grapefruit
3/4 cup Campari
1 bottle Prosecco, fridge cold

Squeeze the grapefruit and mix the juice with the Campari in a large pitcher or cocktail shaker. Stir to combine then slowly add the Prosecco. Pour into champagne glasses. Use the lid to prevent the fizz overflowing as you pour.

Melagrana e prosecco
Pomegranate and prosecco

For 6-8

10 pomegranates, very ripe
1 bottle Prosecco, fridge cold (or
    champagne)

Squeeze the juice from the halved pomegranates as you would oranges or lemons. Fill half a champagne glass with the juice, and top it up with Prosecco or champagne.

Salads
Mozzar
Frittata

ella

2

Zucca gialla intere al forno con pomodori secchi   Pepe
Insalata di fave con pecorino   Insalata di carciofi bo
peperoncino   Coppa con insalata d'inverno e senape
aceto balsamico   Prosciutto con parmigiano e verza
Mozzarella marinata con crème fraîche   Mozzarella
ricotta e maggiorana   Frittata di asparagi e menta
gallinacci

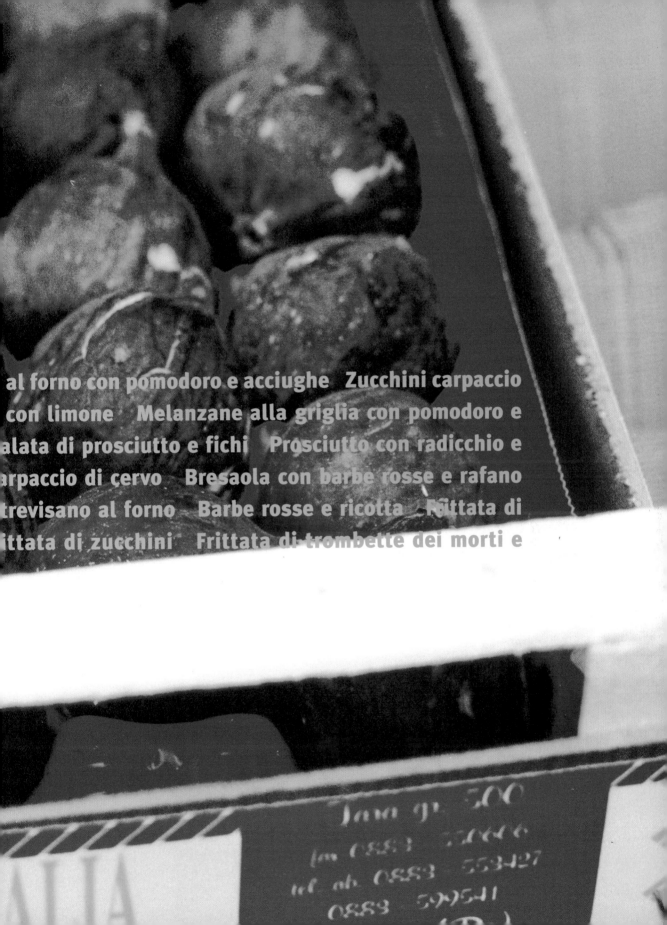

al forno con pomodoro e acciughe Zucchini carpaccio
con limone   Melanzane alla griglia con pomodoro e
alata di prosciutto e fichi   Prosciutto con radicchio e
arpaccio di cervo   Bresaola con barbe rosse e rafano
trevisano al forno   Barbe rosse e ricotta   Frittata di
ittata di zucchini   Frittata di trombette dei morti e

Zucca gialla intere al forno con pomodori secchi
Roasted squashes stuffed with sun-dried tomatoes

For 6 Use pattypan squashes for this recipe as they are portion-size.

6 whole pattypan squashes
12 sun-dried tomatoes, halved, or 1/2 cup whole black olives, pitted
2 garlic cloves, peeled and cut into slivers
1 large bunch fresh thyme, leaves picked from the stalks
2 fresh red chiles, seeded and chopped
olive oil
coarse sea salt and freshly ground black pepper

Preheat the oven to 400° F.

Trim the base of each squash so they stand up. Cut a slice off the top large enough to allow you to scoop out the seeds.

Into each cavity put the sun-dried tomatoes or olives, 2 slivers of garlic, 1 small sprig of thyme, a little chopped chile, and a drizzle of olive oil. Season well with salt and pepper. Place the squashes into an oiled baking dish and cover with foil.

Bake in the preheated oven for 25 minutes. Remove the foil and continue cooking at a lower temperature of 300° F until the flesh is soft, about another 10 minutes.

Peperoni al forno con pomodoro e acciughe
Baked peppers with tomatoes and anchovies

For 6

3 red and 3 yellow peppers
5 tablespoons olive oil
36 cherry tomatoes
3 garlic cloves, peeled and cut into slivers
24 salted anchovy fillets, prepared (see page 346)
1 bunch fresh basil or marjoram
1/2 cup salted capers, prepared (see page 346)
coarse sea salt and freshly ground black pepper

Preheat the oven to 350° F.

Halve each pepper lengthways and remove the core and seeds. Place the peppers in a lightly oiled baking dish, cut side up. Into each half pepper put 3 tomatoes, 2 slivers of garlic, 2 anchovy fillets, a few basil or marjoram leaves, and 3-4 capers. Lightly drizzle the peppers with the remaining olive oil and season with salt and pepper.

Pour about 1 1/3 cups water into the base of the baking dish to prevent the peppers from sticking. Cover the dish tightly with foil. Bake in the preheated oven for 20 minutes, then remove from the oven. Remove the foil, and reduce the oven temperature to 250-300° F, and bake for a further 40 minutes or until the peppers are soft.

Zucchini carpaccio

For 6 Use only small young zucchini for this salad. Good varieties are Gold Rush, Tondo di Nizza, and Bianco Friulano.

2 pounds young yellow and green zucchini
1 bunch arugula
3 tablespoons extra virgin olive oil
juice of 1 lemon
coarse sea salt and freshly ground black pepper
6-ounce piece Parmesan, slivered

Trim the ends off the zucchini and slice at an angle into thin rounds. Place in a bowl.

Pick through the arugula, discarding any yellow leaves. Snap off the stalks, then wash and dry the leaves thoroughly.

Mix together the olive oil, lemon juice, and salt and pepper, and pour over the zucchini. Mix, then leave to marinate for 5 minutes. Season with salt and pepper.

Divide the arugula between the serving plates. Put the zucchini on top, and then the Parmesan slivers. Add a small amount of freshly ground black pepper, and serve.

Insalata di fave con pecorino
Fava bean and pecorino salad

For 6

5 pounds young fava beans in their shells

2 tablespoons aged balsamic vinegar

4 to 6 tablespoons extra virgin olive oil

juice of 1 lemon

coarse sea salt and freshly ground black pepper

1 bunch arugula, leaves picked from the stalks

1 bunch fresh mint, leaves picked from the stalks

5 ounces fresh Pecorino cheese, cut into thin slices

4 ounces aged Pecorino Staginata, or Parmesan, shaved with a vegetable peeler

Shell the fava beans, and separate the larger lighter-colored beans from the smaller greener ones. Bring a large saucepan of water to the boil and blanch the larger beans for 3-5 minutes. Drain and peel off any tough skins.

Combine the raw and the cooked beans in a bowl and add the vinegar, oil, and lemon juice. Toss together and season to taste with salt and pepper.

Combine the arugula and mint in a large bowl, and gently mix in the dressed beans. Layer over this the pieces of both cheeses. Drizzle over a little extra balsamic vinegar and extra virgin olive oil. Serve immediately.

Insalata di carciofi bolliti con limone
Boiled lemon and artichoke heart salad

For 6

4 organic, thick-skinned lemons
6 small or 4 large artichokes with their stems
coarse sea salt and freshly ground black pepper
1 cup almonds, toasted
6 tablespoons raw honey
juice of 2 lemons
1/2 cup extra virgin olive oil
3 tablespoons fresh thyme leaves

Wash the lemons thoroughly, and put 3 of them whole into a small saucepan. Cover with water and add 4 ounces salt. Cover with the lid turned upside down so that the handle keeps the lemons below the surface of the water. Otherwise the lemons will float and not cook properly. Boil for 20 minutes. The lemons will become soft; the skin should easily be pierced with a fork. Drain and cool.

In boiling salted water, to which you have added the halved remaining lemon, cook the artichokes for 20 minutes or until one of the central leaves will come away with a little give. Drain and cool. Pull away the tough outside leaves, trim the stalks of string and fiber, and cut away the choke if there is any. Cut the hearts in halves, or quarters if they are large. Put in a salad bowl and season with salt and pepper.

Cut the boiled lemons in half and scoop out and discard the pulp and inner segments. Cut the soft skins into quarters and add to the artichoke hearts with the almonds.

Mix the honey with the lemon juice, then add the olive oil. Season and pour over the artichokes. Stir in the thyme.

Melanzane alla griglia con pomodoro e peperoncino
Grilled eggplants with tomato-chile paste

For 6

3 large round, pale purple aubergines
extra virgin olive oil
5 garlic cloves, peeled and finely sliced
3 dried red chiles, crumbled
2 tablespoons dried wild oregano
2 28-ounce cans peeled plum tomatoes, drained of their juices (retain the juices)
coarse sea salt and freshly ground black pepper
herb vinegar (Volpaia "Erbe")
3 tablespoons fresh marjoram

Make the tomato-chile paste first. Put 3 tablespoons oil in a heavy-bottomed saucepan, and place over a medium heat. Add the garlic and gently cook until golden, then add the chile and the oregano. Add the tomatoes and mash them into the garlic with a spoon. Stir and cook this pulp over a low heat for at least 45 minutes, stirring from time to time. The tomatoes should thicken and become almost dry. You may add a little of the drained juices if the tomatoes begin to stick. The color should be an intense red and the texture sticky. Season with salt and black pepper and some olive oil. Spread over a flat plate and allow to dry out a bit.

Slice the eggplant 1/4 in thick and grill on a preheated very hot grill pan on both sides. Press to test and see whether they are cooked.

Arrange the slices on a serving plate, drizzle with herb vinegar and olive oil to taste, then spread with the tomato paste. Scatter with the marjoram leaves and serve.

Coppa con insalata d'inverno e senape
Coppa with winter leaves and mustard

For 6

24 very thin slices coppa di Parma

2 bunches arugula

2 heads red or white chicory

1 bunch dandelion leaves

2 heads radicchio

Dressing

3 tablespoons balsamic vinegar

1 1/2 tablespoons Dijon mustard

extra virgin olive oil

coarse sea salt and freshly ground black pepper

Trim all the salad leaves and place in a mixing bowl.

For the dressing, combine the balsamic vinegar and mustard. Thin with olive oil until it is a pourable consistency. Season with salt and pepper.

Toss the salad with half the dressing until each leaf is lightly coated. Divide between six plates in a small pile. Place the slices of coppa on the top and drizzle with the rest of the dressing.

Insalata di prosciutto e fichi
Prosciutto and fig salad

For 6 Ideally you should use purple basil and ripe black figs, or green basil and ripe green figs.

12 slices prosciutto crudo di San Daniele or Parma
9 ripe black or green figs
1 bunch fresh young mint
1 bunch fresh red or green basil
1 bunch arugula
juice of 1 lemon
4-6 tablespoons extra virgin olive oil
coarse sea salt and freshly ground black pepper

Cut the figs in half.

Pick the young tender leaves from the mint, and select the smaller basil leaves. Pick over the arugula, removing the larger stems. Wash and dry.

Mix the lemon juice with the olive oil, and season generously.

Toss the figs with the herbs, arugula, and the dressing. Place on individual plates, combining the prosciutto slices into the salad as you do so.

Prosciutto con radicchio e aceto balsamico
Prosciutto and radicchio with balsamic vinegar

For 6

24 slices prosciutto
3 heads radicchio
10-14-ounce piece Parmesan
2/3 cup extra virgin olive oil
1/2 cup aged balsamic vinegar
1 tablespoon Dijon mustard
1 tablespoon coarse sea salt
1 tablespoon freshly ground black pepper

Remove and discard the outer leaves from the radicchio. Cut each head in half, then, using a large, sharp, and wide-bladed knife, shave into the finest possible shreds. Wash these shreds, then spin dry.

Using a vegetable peeler, or a small sharp knife, shave the Parmesan into slivers.

Mix the olive oil with the balsamic vinegar and mustard, and season to taste with the salt and pepper. Toss the radicchio shreds with the balsamic dressing.

Arrange the slices of prosciutto over each plate and cover with 2-3 tablespoons of the radicchio. Sprinkle with the Parmesan shavings. Drizzle a little extra virgin oil over each plate. Serve immediately.

Prosciutto con parmigiano e verza
Prosciutto, parmesan, and savoy cabbage salad

For 6

24 slices prosciutto
1/2 fresh Savoy cabbage
3/4 cup extra virgin olive oil
coarse sea salt and freshly ground black pepper
2/3 cup aged balsamic vinegar
10-ounce piece Parmesan

Use only the inner, paler leaves from the cabbage and, using a large, sharp, and wide-bladed knife, shave the cabbage into the finest possible shreds. (You do not need to wash, as the inside of a Savoy is so tightly packed.) Place the shreds in a bowl, and add the olive oil and salt and pepper to taste. Toss together, then add the vinegar.

Break the Parmesan into little pieces using a pointed knife. Ease pieces away from the main piece so that they naturally separate along the crystals that form in the cheese. The pieces should be about 1-1 1/4 in long and up to 1/4 in thick. Add to the cabbage mixture and toss.

Arrange the slices of prosciutto over each plate and cover with 2 tablespoons of the cabbage and Parmesan mixture. You could dribble a little extra balsamic vinegar and extra virgin olive oil over each plate. Serve immediately.

Carpaccio di cervo
Venison carpaccio

For 6-8 Use the boned loins and fillets from the saddle of venison. The total weight of the two loins is usually around 1 1/2 pounds.

2 venison loin fillets (see above)
olive oil
coarse sea salt and freshly ground black pepper
1 bunch fresh thyme, leaves picked from the stalks
juice of 2 lemons
1 bunch arugula, washed

Preheat a grill.

Trim the venison loins of any fat and sinew. Brush all over with olive oil and generously season with pepper. Crush the thyme in a pestle and mortar with 2 tablespoons salt. Roll the loins in the crushed mixture. The oil will help the mixture to adhere to the meat.

Place the loins on the hot grill and turn and grill for a few minutes on each side. Do not burn the thyme, just allow the heat from the grill to seal the outside of the meat and form a crust. Allow the meat to cool.

Slice the cold loins as finely as you can. Then, using a very sharp wide-bladed carving knife, place the slices one at a time on a board. Press to flatten with the tip end of the blade, spreading the slice and enlarging it to double its original size.

Arrange the thin lacy slices to cover each plate. Season with salt and pepper, lemon juice, and olive oil, and scatter over a few arugula leaves.

Bresaola con barbe rosse e rafano
Bresaola, beet, and horseradish salad

For 6

12 small young red beets

6 golden beets

2-in piece fresh horseradish

36 thin slices bresaola (6 per person)

5 tablespoons fresh tarragon, leaves picked from the stalks

1/2 cup extra virgin olive oil

juice of 2 lemons

coarse sea salt and freshly ground black pepper

Trim the beet leaves 1 1/4 inches from the bulbs, and gently wash both leaves and bulbs. (Keep the leaves for another dish; see page 60.) Put the bulbs in a saucepan and cover with cold water. Bring to the boil, and simmer for 30 minutes. Test for doneness by pressing a beet between your fingers. Remove the skin – it rubs off very easily. Cut each beet into eighths.

Peel, then grate the horseradish. Use a medium grater which makes mini slivers.

Arrange the bresaola slices over each plate. Divide the beets between the plates over the bresaola. Scatter over the tarragon, then the horseradish. Mix together the oil, lemon juice, and salt and pepper, and pour this dressing over the salad.

Mozzarella marinata con crème fraîche
Marinated mozzarella and crème fraîche

For 6 This is our version of burrata, a southern Italian cheese and cream combination.

1 1/2 pounds fresh mozzarella
coarse sea salt and freshly ground black pepper
extra virgin olive oil
2 tablespoons each of roughly chopped fresh basil, marjoram, mint, and oregano
10 ounces crème fraîche
1 bunch arugula, trimmed
juice of 1 lemon
6 thick slices pugliese or sourdough bruschetta (see page 290)

Cut the mozzarella into 1/4-inch slices. Arrange the cheese on a large flat dish, then season with salt and pepper. Pour over 6 tablespoons of the olive oil and sprinkle over half the fresh chopped herbs. Spoon over the crème fraîche, then turn the cheese slices in this to coat and cover. Sprinkle the remaining herbs on top.

Serve the marinated mozzarella with the bruschetta and the arugula tossed with the lemon juice and some extra virgin olive oil.

Mozzarella con trevisano al forno
Baked mozzarella with radicchio

For 6

1 1/2 pounds fresh mozzarella, cut into 1/2-inch slices

4 heads radicchio

1 bunch fresh marjoram

2 dried red chiles, crumbled

coarse sea salt and freshly ground black pepper

1/4 cup herb vinegar (Volpaia "Erbe") or balsamic vinegar

olive oil

1/2 cup freshly grated Parmesan

1/2 cup pine nuts, lightly toasted

6 thick slices pugliese or sourdough bruschetta (see page 290)

Preheat the oven to 400° F.

Depending on the size of the radicchio heads, cut them into quarters or eighths lengthways; the stem should remain attached to the leaves. Lay the radicchio pieces in a baking tray, and sprinkle with fresh marjoram, chile, salt, pepper, and vinegar, and drizzle with oil. Bake in the preheated oven for 5 minutes.

Place the mozzarella slices over the top of the baked radicchio, then sprinkle with the Parmesan. Place back in the very hot oven until the mozzarella has melted, a few minutes only.

Serve the bruschetta with the radicchio and mozzarella. Sprinkle the toasted pine nuts over the dish as you serve.

Barbe rosse e ricotta
Beet, ricotta, and beet leaf salad

For 6

1 recipe Wood-roasted whole beets (see page 156)

the leaves of the beets

coarse sea salt and freshly ground black pepper

4-6 tablespoons extra virgin olive oil

2 tablespoons herb vinegar (Volpaia "Erbe")

3 fresh red chiles, seeded and finely chopped

1 bunch arugula, washed and dried

1 pound piece fresh ricotta, cut into 6 thin slices

1 small bunch fresh marjoram, leaves picked from the stalks

Sort out the tender leaves from the beets and remove the stalks. Wash carefully and blanch for 2 minutes in boiling salted water. Spread out to drain and cool.

To make the chile sauce, mix together 3 tablespoons of the olive oil and the chile.

Mix together the remaining oil and the vinegar, and season. Cut each beet into halves and halves again. Toss with a few tablespoons of this chile-free dressing.

Divide the arugula between the plates. Toss the blanched beet leaves in the remaining chile-free dressing, and mix with the arugula. Place the quartered beets among the beet leaves and arugula, and cover with the slices of ricotta.

Sprinkle with the marjoram and spoon over a little of the chile sauce.

Frittata di ricotta e maggiorana
Ricotta and marjoram frittata

For 6

8 organic eggs
4 ounces fresh ricotta cheese, lightly beaten with a fork
2 tablespoons chopped fresh marjoram
1/2 cup freshly grated Parmesan
coarse sea salt and freshly ground black pepper
2 tablespoons olive oil

Preheat the oven to 400° F.

Break the eggs into a bowl and beat lightly. Add 3/4 cup of the ricotta, reserving the rest, together with most of the marjoram, most of the Parmesan, and salt and pepper to taste. Stir to combine.

In a small (8-10 in) ovenproof frying pan, heat the olive oil, tilting the pan to coat all sides. Add the egg mixture and lower the heat. Cook over a low heat, loosening the eggs at the sides from time to time, until just set – it should be quite runny.

Scatter with the rest of the marjoram and ricotta, and place in the hot oven for a few seconds only. Loosen the frittata from the pan with a long spatula and put on to a warm plate. Scatter over the remaining Parmesan and cut into wedges to serve.

Frittata di asparagi e menta
Asparagus and mint frittata

For 6

8 organic eggs
8 ounces thin asparagus
coarse sea salt and freshly ground black pepper
1/2 cup freshly grated Parmesan
1 small bunch fresh mint, leaves picked from the stalks, finely chopped
2 tablespoons olive oil

Preheat the oven to 400° F.

Cut off and discard the tough ends of the asparagus, and blanch the spears in boiling water until just tender. Drain, dry, then season with salt and pepper.

Break the eggs into a bowl and beat lightly. Add most of the Parmesan and mint, reserving a little for the end. Season with salt and pepper to taste.

Cook the frittata in the ovenproof frying pan as opposite. Just before placing it in the hot oven, put the asparagus and the remaining Parmesan and mint on top. Serve as opposite.

Frittata di zucchini
Zucchini frittata

For 6

8 organic eggs
4 small or 3 medium zucchini
3 tablespoons olive oil
2 garlic cloves, peeled and chopped
1 small bunch fresh basil, leaves picked from the stalks and roughly chopped
coarse sea salt and freshly ground black pepper
1/2 cup freshly grated Parmesan

Preheat the oven to 400° F.

Trim the zucchini, then cut thinly at an angle. Heat 2 tablespoons of the oil in an ovenproof frying pan. Add the garlic followed by the zucchini slices. When brown on all sides, add most of the basil and salt and pepper to taste. The zucchini should be quite dry; if there is any oil remaining, drain through a sieve and reserve.

Break the eggs into a bowl and beat lightly. Add the zucchini and garlic, reserving 1 tablespoon for the end. Season with salt and pepper.

Cook the frittata in the ovenproof frying pan as on page 44, using the reserved oil as well as the remaining 1 tablespoon if necessary. Just before placing it into the hot oven, spread the rest of the zucchini on top. Remove from the oven and sprinkle with the Parmesan and the remaining basil. Serve as on page 44.

Frittata di trombette dei morti e gallinacci
Trompettes de mort and girolles frittata

For 6

8 organic eggs

12 ounces trompettes de mort (or other mushrooms)

8 ounces chanterelles (or other mushrooms)

3 tablespoons olive oil

2 garlic cloves, peeled and thinly sliced

a handful of chopped fresh basil or parsley

coarse sea salt and freshly ground black pepper

1/4 cup freshly grated Parmesan

Cut off the stalk end of the trompettes. Wash the trompettes by plunging them briefly into cold water and dry in a salad spinner. Cut off the stalk ends of the chanterelles. Clean with a brush.

Heat 2 tablespoons of the olive oil in a pan and add the garlic. Cook quickly until tender, then remove from the pan and drain. Retain the oil and return it to the pan. Add the chanterelles and fry for a minute or two, then add the trompettes and cook for a further few minutes. Add the basil or parsley, and salt and pepper to taste.

Break the eggs into a bowl and beat lightly. Add three-quarters of the mushroom mixture, and season with salt and pepper.

Cook the frittata in the ovenproof frying pan as on page 44, using the reserved oil as well as the remaining 2 tablespoons if necessary. Just before placing it into the hot oven, put the rest of the mushrooms on top, along with the Parmesan. Serve as on page 44.

Past
Pole

a
nta

Pasta all'uovo   Pasta verde   Ravioli di patate e rucola
Rotolo verde con ricotta e erbe d'estiva   Tagliatelle co
Pappardelle con cavolo nero e lenticchie   Zucchini ca
bianchi   Spaghetti con rucola e ricotta   Linguini con f
con cozze delle marche   Spaghetti alle vongole   Sp
Penne con zucchini e ricotta   Bucatini con acciughe
Polenta con tartufi bianchi   Polenta con porcini fresch

Ravioli ripiene di bietole   Ravioli di zucca e mascarpone

mascarpone e pangrattato   Tagliatelle con salsa di noci

onara   Tagliatelle con gallinacci   Tagliatelle con tartufi

ve fresche   Spaghetti con aragosta marinata   Spaghetti

ghettini con calamari   Penne con broccoli e olive verdi

pangrattato   Polenta in brodo di pollo con cavolo nero

Pasta all'uovo
Fresh Pasta

Makes about 2 1/4 pounds This is easiest to make in a large-capacity food processor. If you have a smaller food processor, make it in two batches.

4 cups all-purpose flour
1 cup cake flour (not self-rising)
1 tablespoon fine sea salt
1 tablespoon extra-virgin olive oil
9 large egg yolks
6 large eggs
semolina (pasta flour), for dusting

In a large food processor, pulse the all-purpose flour, cake flour, and salt to combine. Add the oil. In a large glass measuring cup, mix the yolks and whole eggs. With the machine running, gradually pour the egg mixture through the feed tube until the dough forms a ball on top of the blade. (Depending on the flour, you may not need all of the egg mixture, or you may have to add another egg yolk.) Gather up the dough, then cut into two portions, and form each into a ball. Keeping the other ball covered with plastic wrap, knead each ball on a semolina-dusted surface until smooth, 3 to 4 minutes. Wrap each ball tightly in plastic wrap. Refrigerate until chilled, 1 1/2 to 2 hours.

Divide each ball into 3 portions. Work with 1 portion at a time, keeping the others covered. Dust with flour and pass through the widest setting of a pasta machine. Fold the sheet into thirds, and pass through ten more times, until silky. Set the machine to the next setting, and repeat the rolling and folding for six more times. Repeat at the third setting for six more times. Continue rolling (but not folding) the pasta for four times per setting until you reach the desired thickness (usually the second-to-last setting for tagliatelle, or thinner for ravioli).

Pasta verde
Spinach Pasta

Makes about 2 3/4 pounds

1 1/2 pounds young, tender spinach
4 cups all-purpose flour
1 cup cake flour (not self-rising)
1 tablespoon fine sea salt
13 large egg yolks
2 large eggs
semolina flour, for dusting

Cut off and discard the tough stems from the spinach leaves. Rinse the leaves well. Drain. In a large saucepan, bring 1/2 cup water to a boil over medium heat. Add the spinach and cover tightly. Cook until the spinach is tender, about 5 minutes. Drain and rinse under cold water. A handful at a time, squeeze the excess water out of the spinach. Chop finely and set aside.

In a large food processor, pulse the all-purpose flour, cake flour, and salt to combine. Add the spinach. In a large glass measuring cup, mix the yolks and whole eggs. With the machine running, gradually pour the egg mixture through the feed tube until the dough forms a ball on top of the blade. (You may not need all of the egg mixture, or you may have to add another egg yolk. If your food processor is normal capacity, you may have to make the dough in two batches.) Gather up the dough, then cut into two portions, and form each into a ball. Keeping the other ball covered with plastic wrap, knead each ball on a semolina-dusted surface until smooth, 3 to 4 minutes. Wrap each ball tightly in plastic wrap. Refrigerate until chilled, 1 1/2 to 2 hours.

Prepare the dough as for Fresh Pasta.

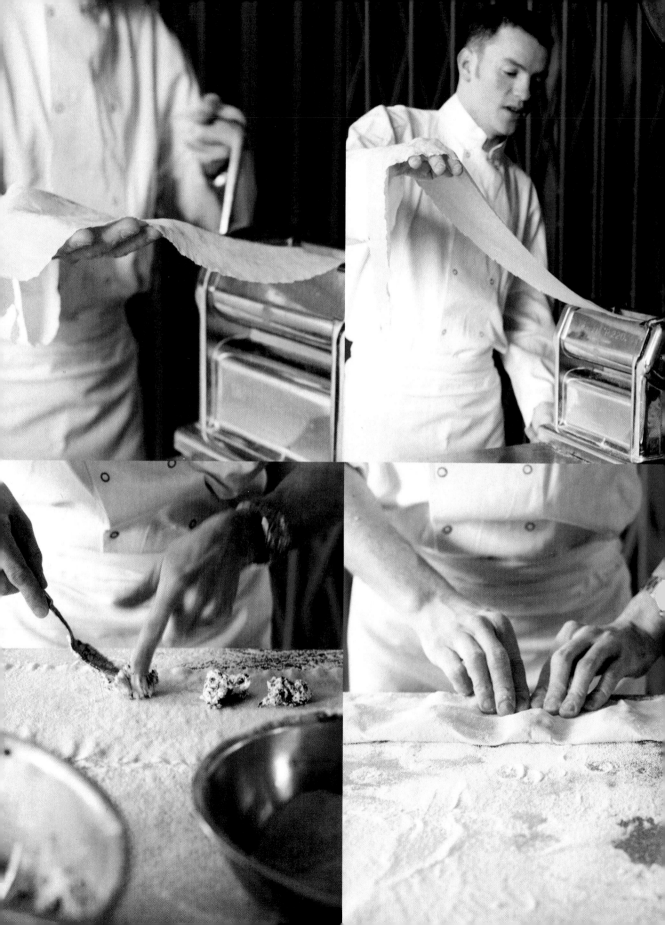

Ravioli di patate e rucola
Ravioli with potato and arugula

For 8 Use Pecorino Romano, a salty sheep's milk cheese with the same crystalline formation as Parmesan.

1 recipe Fresh Pasta (see page 54)

semolina flour for dusting

4 to 6 tablespoons extra virgin olive oil

1/2 cup freshly grated Pecorino Romano

1/2 pound arugula, washed, dried, and roughly chopped

Filling

4 1/2 pounds small red potatoes, scrubbed clean (do not peel)

coarse sea salt and freshly ground black pepper

3-4 tablespoons extra virgin olive oil

4 garlic cloves, peeled and finely chopped

2-3 small dried red chiles, crumbled

2 1/2 pounds arugula, washed and dried

1 cup freshly grated Pecorino Romano

Boil the potatoes in salted water until soft. Cool. Scrape off and discard the skin, and put the flesh through the coarse blade of a food mill.

Heat the oil in a large heavy-bottomed pan and fry the garlic and chile until the garlic is just turning gold. Add 1 3/4 pounds of the arugula, stir briefly, then put on the lid and immediately remove from the heat. This allows the arugula to wilt in the steam generated. Cool, then drain off excess liquid and chop the arugula finely.

Roughly chop the remaining raw arugula for the filling.

In a large cold mixing bowl mix together the mashed potato, the chopped wilted arugula, the chopped raw arugula, and the Pecorino. Season with black pepper and salt to taste (but be sparing with the latter as the Pecorino is salty).

Divide the pasta into balls the size of a large egg. Using a pasta machine, roll them out into long strips (one at a time to prevent drying) as thin as possible. Cut in half if too long.

Put tablespoons of filling about 2 1/4 in apart on the sheet, in the center of the half nearest you, so that you can fold the other half over to make a "parcel" of about 2 in square. Brush around the fillings with a pastry brush dipped in water before folding, so that the envelopes you are making will seal properly. Using a pasta cutter, seal each envelope by cutting on three sides (the fourth is the fold). Dust a large plate or tray with semolina flour and carefully place the ravioli on it, making sure that they do not touch. You should have about fifty.

Bring a large pan of salted water to the boil, and put in the ravioli. Lower heat to a simmer: the ravioli will rise to the surface of the water after 30 seconds, but according to how thin you managed to roll the pasta, they will take from 3-5 minutes to cook. Test where the joined pasta is thickest; it should be al dente.

Serve the ravioli with a drizzle of extra virgin olive oil, grated Pecorino, and a scattering of chopped fresh arugula.

Ravioli ripiene di bietole
Ravioli with beet leaves

For 8

1 recipe Fresh Pasta (see page 54)

semolina flour for dusting

Sage Butter (see opposite)

Filling

1 pound tender leaves from young beets, stalks removed

coarse sea salt and freshly ground black pepper

1 small red onion, peeled and finely chopped

2 tablespoons unsalted butter

1 bunch fresh marjoram, leaves picked from the stalks

1 garlic clove, peeled and finely chopped

5 ounces ricotta cheese, lightly broken up with a fork

1 cup grated Parmesan

1/2 teaspoon freshly grated nutmeg

Wash the beet leaves and blanch in salted water for 4 minutes. Drain and lay out on a tray to dry. Chop finely.

Gently fry the onion in the butter in a large heavy-bottomed pan until the onion begins to brown. Add the marjoram and garlic, stir for 1 minute, then add the beet leaves. Just cook together briefly, season, and allow to cool.

Stir the beet leaves and Parmesan into the ricotta. Add nutmeg and season.

Make the ravioli as described in the previous recipe. Serve with Sage Butter.

Ravioli di zucca e mascarpone
Ravioli with pumpkin and mascarpone

For 8

1 recipe Fresh Pasta (see page 54)

semolina flour for dusting

Filling

about 3 pounds, pumpkin or squash, cooked (see page 158)

4 tablespoons unsalted butter

2 large garlic cloves, peeled and finely sliced

1 bunch fresh marjoram, leaves picked from the stalks

coarse sea salt and freshly ground black pepper

18 ounces mascarpone cheese

2 cups freshly grated Parmesan

1/2 nutmeg, freshly grated

Sage butter

2 bunches fresh sage, leaves picked from the stalks

7 ounces unsalted butter, clarified

Cool the cooked pumpkin or squash, discard the skin, and mash the flesh. In a heavy-bottomed saucepan, melt the butter and cook the garlic until golden. Add the marjoram and the mashed pumpkin, combine, and taste for seasoning. When cool, stir in the mascarpone, Parmesan, and nutmeg.

Make the ravioli as in the potato ravioli recipe. For the sage butter, heat the clarified butter in a small pan and, when hot, add the sage leaves for a second or two. Remove from the heat.

Cook the ravioli as in the potato ravioli recipe, then serve with the sage butter.

Rotolo verde con ricotta e erbe d'estiva
Spinach pasta with ricotta and summer herbs

For 6

1 recipe Spinach Pasta (see page 55)
coarse sea salt and freshly ground black pepper
semolina flour for dusting
Parmesan, freshly grated

Olive paste

1 cup pitted black Niçoise olives
2 garlic cloves, peeled
3 tablespoons fresh basil
3 tablespoons fresh marjoram

Filling

1 1/2 pounds ricotta cheese
1 1/4 cups freshly grated Parmesan
1/4 cup chopped fresh basil
3 tablespoons chopped fresh marjoram
3 tablespoons chopped fresh parsley
3 organic eggs
1/2 cup cream

Nutmeg butter

4 ounces (1 stick) unsalted butter, clarified
1 teaspoon freshly grated nutmeg

To make the olive paste, put the olives, garlic, basil, and marjoram into the bowl of a food processor and pulse-chop. Remove to a bowl and set aside.

To make the filling, beat the ricotta with a fork to lighten and separate it. Add the Parmesan, the basil, marjoram, and parsley, and season with salt and pepper to taste. Take about half of this herb ricotta and place in the (cleaned) bowl of the food processor. Pulse-chop to combine and then add the eggs one by one. Finally add the cream and mix in. You will have a bright green, fairly liquid mixture. Carefully fold this mixture into the remaining ricotta mix to combine, and then season to taste.

Roll the pasta out by hand on a work surface dusted with semolina flour to a large sheet, as thin as possible; it will not matter if there are a few holes or tears. Cut the edges to straighten; you should have a piece of about 12 in square.

If you have a pasta machine, roll out two strips and join to make the same size by brushing the edges with water to seal.

Spread the olive paste along the edge of the side nearest you, and then spread the ricotta mixture over the rest of the sheet to a 1/2 in thickness. Scatter with a little grated Parmesan. Starting with the olive edge, gently roll the pasta up into a large sausage, about 2 1/2 in thick. Wrap the roll in a large tea towel as tightly as you can, securing with string to help keep the roll in shape. (If you do not have a fish poacher, the best cooking pot for this long roll, you will have to cut the roll in half and make two tea towel–wrapped parcels.)

Fill the fish kettle or other suitable pan with water and bring to the boil. Add salt generously and poach the pasta roll for about 20-25 minutes.

Meanwhile, make the nutmeg butter. After clarifying the butter, grate the whole nutmeg into it, and season with salt and pepper. Heat gently.

Drain the pasta roll and remove from the cloth. Place on a board and cut into generous 3/4-in slices. Ladle the nutmeg butter over, and sprinkle with some grated Parmesan.

Tagliatelle con mascarpone e pangrattato

For 6 as a starter

1 1/2 pounds fresh tagliatelle (see page 54) or 1 pound dried egg tagliatelle

1 pound mascarpone cheese

4 organic egg yolks

1/2 cup extra virgin olive oil

4 garlic cloves, peeled and finely chopped

1 1/4 cups freshly grated Parmesan

coarse sea salt and freshly ground black pepper

Herb pangrattato

1 loaf Italian-style bread, bottom crust removed, made into coarse crumbs

1/2 cup extra virgin olive oil

6 garlic cloves, peeled and left whole

3 tablespoons each of chopped fresh thyme and marjoram

Slowly mix the mascarpone and egg yolks together in a food processor. Add the oil, drop by drop, as for mayonnaise. Stir in the chopped garlic and Parmesan. Season.

Heat the oil for the pangrattato in a small saucepan and add the whole garlic cloves. Cook gently until a deep golden color, then remove the cloves. Add the bread crumbs to the garlic-flavored oil and cook until golden. Just before they turn brown, add the herbs. Immediately remove the bread crumbs and herbs from the oil using a slotted spoon, and drain on paper towels.

Cook the tagliatelle in a large pan of boiling salted water until al dente, then drain. Mix with the mascarpone and generously cover with the herb pangrattato.

Tagliatelle con salsa di noci
Tagliatelle with walnut sauce

For 6 as a starter

1 1/2 pounds fresh tagliatelle or 1 pound dried egg tagliatelle

4 1/2 pounds green walnuts, shelled and bitter skins removed

bread crumbs from 1 loaf Italian-style bread, stale if possible, soaked in 2/3 cup milk

3 garlic cloves, peeled

coarse sea salt and freshly ground black pepper

2 tablespoons roughly chopped fresh flat-leaf parsley

1/2 cup olive oil

1/2 cup freshly grated Parmesan

1/4 cup roughly chopped fresh basil

4 tablespoons soft unsalted butter

Keeping a few pieces of walnut whole for serving, pound the remainder together with the garlic in a mortar. Add a little salt and then the parsley, and continue to pound.

Squeeze most of the milk from the bread crumbs (reserve the milk). Add half of the bread crumbs to the mortar, and mix in. Add the olive oil gradually, plus a little of the milk to loosen the paste, stirring continuously; the sauce must be well amalgamated. Finally, add half the Parmesan and basil, then season. The result is a thick green sauce.

Cook the tagliatelle in a generous amount of boiling salted water, then drain thoroughly and return to the saucepan. Add the softened butter and stir in the sauce.

Serve with the rest of the basil, Parmesan, and a few pieces of uncrushed walnut.

Pappardelle con cavolo nero e lenticchie
Pappardelle with cavolo nero and lentils

For 6 as a starter

3 heads cavolo nero, stalks removed, blanched and roughly chopped
   (or equivalent amount kale)
2 tablespoons olive oil
4 ounces pancetta, cut into matchsticks
1 small red onion, peeled and finely sliced
1/2 head celery, stalks and leaves chopped
1 teaspoon chopped fresh rosemary leaves
1 garlic clove, peeled
1/2 cup Chianti Classico wine
2/3 cup Chicken Stock (see page 142)
coarse sea salt and freshly ground black pepper
1 cup Castelluccio or Puy lentils, cooked (see page 347)
1 1/2 pounds fresh pappardelle or 1 pound dried
1/2 cup freshly grated Parmesan
extra virgin olive oil

Heat the oil in a heavy-bottomed pan and fry the pancetta slowly to release the fat, then add the onion and celery. Cook until they begin to color, then add the rosemary and garlic, and fry for 5 minutes. Add the wine and cook briefly until reduced.

Heat the stock. Add the lentils to the pancetta mixture, stir, and cook to combine for 3-4 minutes. Add the cavolo and enough stock to liquefy the mixture. Season with salt and pepper. Heat through.

Cook the pappardelle then drain well. Mix into the lentil mixture, then add the Parmesan. Toss and serve with oil drizzled over and sprinkled with the celery leaves.

Zucchini carbonara
Tagliatelle with deep-fried zucchini

For 6 as a starter

2 pounds small young fresh zucchini, trimmed

1 cup olive oil

1 1/2 pounds fresh tagliatelle or 1 pound dried egg tagliatelle

coarse sea salt and freshly ground black pepper

1 small dried red chile, crumbled

5 medium organic eggs, lightly beaten

1 cup grated Pecorino

1 bunch fresh basil, cut into ribbons

Cut the zucchini into fine dice. Heat the olive oil in a heavy-bottomed pan, and when hot fry the diced zucchini in batches, one layer at a time. They take seconds to brown on the edges and become crisp. Remove and drain on paper towels.

Cook the pasta in a generous amount of boiling salted water, then drain thoroughly. Season with salt and pepper and the crumbled dried chile, and return to the hot saucepan. Add the beaten eggs and stir to combine, allowing the egg to cook just by contact with the hot pasta. Add the zucchini dice, half the Pecorino, and the basil. Serve with the remaining grated Pecorino on top.

Tagliatelle con gallinacci
Tagliatelle with girolles

For 6 as a starter

1 1/2 pounds fresh tagliatelle (see page 54) or 1 pound dried tagliatelle

2 pounds fresh girolles (or other mushrooms)

3 tablespoons olive oil

4 garlic cloves, peeled and finely chopped

juice of 1 lemon

coarse sea salt and freshly ground black pepper

1 bunch fresh flat-leaf parsley, leaves picked from the stalks, finely chopped

1/2 cup unsalted butter, softened

1/2 cup grated Parmesan

Pick through the girolles, brushing out any leaves or moss, or bits of earth or sand. Trim the stalks. Tear them in halves, quarters, or eighths lengthways, according to size, so that the stalks remain attached to the cups. You are aiming to echo the width of the tagliatelle with the pieces of girolle.

Heat the olive oil in a pan until smoking, then add the girolles and toss. Add the garlic and cook over a high heat for a minute or two. Add the lemon juice, and season with salt, pepper, and parsley.

Cook the tagliatelle in a generous amount of boiling salted water until al dente, then drain. Add the butter, girolles, and Parmesan to the tagliatelle and serve with extra Parmesan.

Tagliatelle con tartufi bianchi
Tagliatelle with white truffles

For 6 as a starter

1 1/2 pounds fresh tagliatelle or 1 pound dried egg tagliatelle
white truffles, 1 ounce per person
coarse sea salt and freshly ground black pepper
6 ounces unsalted butter, softened
3 tablespoons grated Parmesan

Clean the truffles with a soft brush to remove all sand and grit. If there is any clay clinging, use a small pointed knife to scrape it off. Never use water.

Cook the pasta in a generous amount of boiling salted water, then drain thoroughly, saving a little of the water. Stir in three-quarters of the softened butter and a few tablespoons of the pasta water. Season with salt and pepper, add the Parmesan, and toss together.

Grate the first few shavings from each truffle into the pasta, and toss. Serve on warm plates, and place a little knob of the softened remaining butter on top. Generously shave the truffles all over each portion. Serve with extra Parmesan.

Spaghetti con rucola e ricotta
Spaghetti with arugula and ricotta

For 6 as a starter

2 1/4 pounds arugula

6 tablespoons extra virgin olive oil

3 garlic cloves, peeled and roughly chopped

1/4 cup fresh basil leaves, torn into pieces

2 fresh red chiles, seeded and chopped

coarse sea salt and freshly ground black pepper

1 pound spaghetti

7 ounces ricotta, lightly beaten with a fork

1 1/4 cups Parmesan, grated

Wash the arugula and dry in a salad spinner. Divide the quantity in half, and roughly chop one of these halves.

Heat a large saucepan and add 2 tablespoons of the oil. Gently fry the garlic until it begins to turn gold, then add the torn-up basil leaves and the whole arugula. Put on the lid and let the arugula wilt – this takes 2-3 minutes. Put the hot wilted arugula and any liquid in the pan in a food processor and pulse-chop. Add half of the chopped arugula and blend again to combine. Stir in the chiles, salt, pepper, and the remaining olive oil.

Cook the spaghetti in plenty of boiling salted water. Drain, return to the pan, and add the arugula sauce. Turn the pasta over gently to coat each strand. Finally, lightly fork in the ricotta and the remaining chopped arugula. Season, and serve with the Parmesan.

Linguini con fave fresche
Linguine with fresh fava beans

For 6 as a starter Make this pasta only when fava beans are young and tender.

2 cups shelled fava beans

1 small red onion, peeled and finely chopped

2 garlic cloves, peeled and finely chopped

1 small bunch fresh parsley, chopped

3 tablespoons olive oil

1 cup hot water

1 pound linguine

coarse sea salt and freshly ground black pepper

1/2 cup freshly grated Parmesan

In a large heavy saucepan cook the onion, garlic, and parsley slowly in the oil for 5 minutes or until very soft. Add the fava beans and stir for several minutes. Add the water and cook until the beans are tender. Add salt and pepper. Put half of the beans in the food processor and pulse-chop to a coarse purée. Return to and mix with the whole beans.

Cook the linguine in plenty of boiling salted water until al dente. Drain, then add to the sauce and stir. Check for seasoning and serve with the Parmesan.

Spaghetti con aragosta marinata
Marinated lobster spaghetti

For 6 We use lobster culls, which are usually much cheaper. Serve this pasta as a main course.

6 1 pound lobsters, or 3 large or 3-4 medium lobsters

coarse sea salt and freshly ground black pepper

3 bay leaves

1 large fresh red chile

1 head garlic

1 pound 6 ounces spaghetti

1 bunch flat-leaf parsley, leaves picked from the stalks, chopped

3 lemons, halved

Marinade

2 garlic cloves, peeled

juice of 3 lemons

1/2 cup extra virgin olive oil

1 small dried red chile, crumbled

Put the lobsters in a very large saucepan of cold salted water. They should be completely covered. Use two saucepans if necessary. Add the bay, fresh chile, and garlic to the water, and place the pan over a low heat. Bring to the boil very slowly.

When the water has come to the boil, take the lobsters out and allow to cool. Remove all the meat from the shells, dividing the bodies into two or three large pieces each.

For the marinade, crush the garlic with a teaspoon of sea salt, and add to the lemon juice and olive oil. Season with salt and pepper and the dried chile. Marinate the lobster pieces for 30 minutes.

Cook the spaghetti in a generous amount of boiling salted water, then drain and return to the pan. Add the lobster and marinade. Heat through, stir in the parsley, season, and serve with lemon halves.

Spaghetti con cozze delle marche
Spaghetti with mussels

For 6 as a starter

6 pounds mussels, cleaned

1/4 cup olive oil

3 garlic cloves, peeled and chopped

1 small dried red chile, crumbled

2 tablespoons chopped fresh oregano

1/2 cup white wine (Verdicchio Classico)

2 pounds ripe tomatoes, skinned, seeded, and chopped

coarse sea salt and freshly ground black pepper

3 tablespoons chopped fresh flat-leaf parsley

1 pound spaghetti

extra virgin olive oil

In a large heavy saucepan with a tight-fitting lid, heat half the olive oil. Add the mussels, cover, and cook briefly over a high heat until all open, about 5 minutes. Discard any still closed. Drain, retaining the liquid. When the mussels are cool remove from their shells and chop. Reduce the liquid by half, strain, and add to the mussels.

In a separate large pan heat the remainder of the oil, add the garlic, chile, and oregano, and cook briefly until the garlic begins to color. Add the wine, reduce for a minute, then add the tomatoes. Cook, stirring to prevent sticking, for 15 minutes until reduced. Add the mussels, juice, seasoning, and parsley. Heat up the sauce.

Cook the spaghetti in a generous amount of boiling salted water, then drain. Add to the sauce. To serve, pour over extra virgin olive oil.

Spaghetti alle vongole
Spaghetti with clams

For 6 as a starter The smallest and sweetest clams are what you want when using them as a sauce for thin spaghetti.

6 pounds small clams, washed

1/4 cup extra virgin olive oil

4 garlic cloves, peeled and finely chopped

3 dried red chiles, crumbled

1/3 cup white wine (Sauvignon)

coarse sea salt and freshly ground black pepper

1 bunch fresh flat-leaf parsley, finely chopped

1 pound spaghetti

3 lemons, cut into quarters

Heat the olive oil in a large heavy saucepan, add the garlic, and cook for a minute until just beginning to color. Add the crumbled chile and the clams, cover with the lid, and cook the clams over a high heat to open them, about 2-3 minutes. Remove the clams with a slotted spoon. (Discard any that have not opened.) Remove half of the clams from their shells, and discard the shells. Keep all to one side.

Add the white wine to the hot juices remaining in the pan and, keeping the heat high, reduce for 3-4 minutes. The sauce should be sweet and slightly thick. Season with pepper and some salt if necessary; the clams may be salty. Add half of the parsley and all the clams back into the sauce.

Cook the spaghetti in a generous amount of boiling salted water, then drain and add to the clam sauce. Serve with the remaining parsley and lemon quarters.

Spaghettini con calamari
Squid spaghettini

For 6 as a starter

8 medium squid, no larger than your hand

1 pound spaghettini

coarse sea salt and freshly ground black pepper

5 tablespoons olive oil

3 garlic cloves, peeled and finely chopped

3 fresh red chiles, seeded and finely chopped

1/3 white wine

1 small bunch fresh flat-leaf parsley, finely chopped

Put a large pan of salted water on to boil.

Meanwhile, clean the squid by pulling the tentacles and heads away from the bodies. Keep the tentacles together. Remove the eyes and mouth. Cut the body open so it is flat, and scrape out the guts. Slice the body into thin strips about 1/2 in thick. Cut the bunches of tentacles in half.

Cook the spaghettini in the boiling salted water until al dente, about 7 minutes. Remove and drain well.

Meanwhile, heat the oil in a saucepan over a high flame and quickly fry the garlic. In a matter of seconds it should begin to color. Now add the chopped chiles and fry for a few seconds more, then add the squid strips and tentacles. Cook for about half a minute. Pour in the white wine, allow the alcohol to evaporate, and then add half the chopped parsley, and salt and black pepper.

Toss the squid sauce well with the spaghettini and serve with the rest of the parsley.

Penne con broccoli e olive verdi
Penne with broccoli and green olives

For 6 as a starter

2 pounds broccoli, florets and small leaves only

coarse sea salt and freshly ground black pepper

2 small red onions, peeled and finely sliced

1/4 cup extra virgin olive oil

2 garlic cloves, peeled and sliced

16 salted anchovy fillets, prepared (see page 346)

1 cup pine nuts, toasted

1 cup green olives, pitted and halved

1 pound penne

1 cup grated Pecorino

1/2 cup roughly torn fresh basil

Cut the broccoli florets into small pieces, and blanch with the leaves for 5 minutes. Drain well (reserve the blanching water).

In a heavy-bottomed saucepan, gently fry the onion until golden in 2 tablespoons of the olive oil. Add the garlic and anchovy fillets, and stir to break up the anchovies; they will melt into a sauce. Add 1 ladleful of blanching water. Add the broccoli, cook for 5 minutes, then add the pine nuts and olive pieces and continue to cook over a gentle heat for 5 minutes to combine all the flavors. Season.

Cook the penne in boiling salted water, then drain. Add to the sauce along with the basil, Pecorino, and remaining olive oil and serve.

Penne con zucchini e ricotta
Penne with zucchini and ricotta

For 6 as a starter

2 pounds small young zucchini
coarse sea salt and freshly ground black pepper
2 tablespoons olive oil
4 garlic cloves, peeled and chopped
1 pound penne
12 ounces ricotta cheese
1 bunch fresh basil, shredded
1/2 cup freshly grated Parmesan

Trim the zucchini, then blanch whole in boiling salted water for about 2 minutes. Drain, cool, and slice at an angle, about 1/2 in thick.

In a large heavy saucepan heat the olive oil and cook the garlic until very soft but not brown. Add the zucchini slices and toss over a low heat for 4-5 minutes.

Cook the penne in plenty of boiling salted water, then drain well. Add to the zucchini, then crumble in the ricotta. Season, toss together, and add the basil and Parmesan.

Bucatini con acciughe e pangrattato
Bucatini with anchovies and pangrattato

For 6 as a starter

1/3 cup olive oil

3 garlic cloves, peeled and thinly sliced

3 dried red chiles, crumbled

18 salted anchovy fillets, prepared (see page 346) and roughly chopped

coarse sea salt and freshly ground black pepper

zest and juice of 2 lemons

1 pound bucatini

1 small bunch fresh flat-leaf parsley, finely chopped

Pangrattato

2 cups olive oil

10 garlic cloves, peeled and kept whole

1 loaf Italian-style bread, bottom crust removed, made into coarse crumbs

Make the Pangrattato. Heat the oil in a small saucepan and add the garlic. Cook over a medium heat until the garlic turns golden, then discard. Add the bread crumbs to the pan and cook until crisp and golden. Drain on paper towels then season.

Heat the oil in a saucepan and gently fry the garlic until it begins to color. Add a third of the chile and the anchovies, and stir to combine. Remove from the heat. Add the lemon juice and black pepper.

Cook the bucatini in plenty of boiling salted water and drain. Add to the anchovy sauce. Serve on individual plates and sprinkle with lemon zest, the remaining chile, the pangrattato, and the parsley.

Polenta in brodo di pollo con cavolo nero
Wet polenta with chicken stock and cavolo nero

For 6

9 ounces coarse-ground cornmeal

8 heads cavolo nero (or equivalent amount kale)

coarse sea salt and freshly ground black pepper

4 garlic cloves, peeled

5-6 cups Chicken Stock, well seasoned (see page 142)

4-6 tablespoons unsalted butter

1 cup grated Parmesan

Put a large pan of water on to boil for blanching the cavolo, and season it with salt.

Prepare the cavolo nero by removing any large discolored or tough outer leaves. Remove the central stems and discard. Wash the leaves well, then blanch with the garlic for 5 minutes until tender. Drain and pulse-chop the cavolo and garlic in the food processor. Season.

Put the polenta in a measuring cup so that it can be poured in a steady stream. Bring the Chicken Stock to a simmer in a large heavy-bottomed saucepan; it should come halfway up the sides of the pan. Pour the polenta into the stock slowly in a continuous stream, and, using a long-handled whisk, whisk constantly so that lumps do not form, until completely blended. The polenta will start to bubble volcanically. Reduce the heat to low and cook, stirring with a spoon to prevent a skin forming on the top, for about 40-45 minutes. The polenta is cooked when it falls away from the sides of the pan. Stir in the butter, the Parmesan, the cavolo nero, black pepper, and some salt if needed.

Polenta con tartufi bianchi
Wet polenta with fresh white truffles

For 6

12 ounces coarse-ground cornmeal
7 1/2-9 cups water
coarse sea salt and freshly ground black pepper
6 ounces (1 1/2 sticks) unsalted butter, softened
6-ounce piece Parmesan
5-6 ounces white truffle, carefully brushed clean

Put the polenta flour in a large pitcher so that it can be poured in a steady stream. Bring the water to a boil in a large heavy-bottomed saucepan; it should come halfway up the sides of the pan. Add 1 teaspoon of salt and then slowly add the polenta flour in a continuous stream, stirring with a long-handled whisk all the time (so that lumps do not form) until completely blended. The polenta will start to bubble volcanically. Reduce the heat to as low as possible and cook, stirring with a spoon to prevent a skin forming on the top, for about 40-45 minutes. The polenta is cooked when it falls away from the sides of the pan. Stir in 2 ounces of the butter and 4 ounces of the Parmesan, grated.

Divide the polenta between the plates, and season with salt and pepper. Mash the remaining butter with a spoon, and spread a little over each portion. Grate or shave the remaining Parmesan directly on top, then finally cover completely with fine shavings of white truffle, as much as you can afford: a generous helping would be about 6 ounces for six people.

Polenta con porcini freschi
Wet polenta with fresh porcini

For 6-8

4 1/2 pounds fresh porcini mushrooms, brushed clean and cut into 2-in slices

12 ounces coarse-ground cornmeal

7 1/2-9 cups water

coarse sea salt and freshly ground black pepper

7 ounces unsalted butter, softened

1 cup grated Parmesan

3 tablespoons olive oil

2 garlic cloves, peeled and thinly sliced

1 small dried red chile, crumbled

juice of 1 lemon

1/4 cup roughly chopped fresh flat-leaf parsley

Make the Wet Polenta as in the previous recipe. When cooked, stir in 2 ounces of the soft butter, half the grated Parmesan, black pepper, and some salt if needed.

Heat the oil and the remaining butter together in a large frying pan until almost smoking. Add the mushrooms and fry quickly, turning the slices over so that they brown evenly. Add the garlic, and stir it into the mushrooms; it will cook very quickly. Season generously with the dried chile, salt, and pepper, and finally add the lemon juice and the parsley.

Serve the Wet Polenta with the remaining Parmesan sprinkled over each serving before you spoon over the mushrooms.

otto

4

Risotto di asparagi Risotto con ricotta e basilico R
erbe Risotto con funghi di bosco Risotto al rosmar
granchio Risotto con trevisano e pancetta Risotto co

e bisi   Risotto verde con pancetta   Risotto verde alle
o   Risotto con finocchio e vodka   Risotto con porcini
artufi bianchi   Risotto al limone con basilico

Risotto di asparagi
Asparagus risotto

For 6

2 pounds asparagus, trimmed

1 quart Chicken Stock (see page 142)

coarse sea salt and freshly ground black pepper

1 small red onion, peeled and very finely chopped

2 tablespoons unsalted butter

3 tablespoons olive oil

1 1/2 cups risotto rice

1/3 cup vermouth

3/4 cup grated Parmesan

Heat the Chicken Stock and check for seasoning.

Cut the tips off the asparagus and keep to one side. Chop the tender parts of the stalks into approximately 1 in pieces.

Blanch the asparagus tips for 2 minutes, then blanch the stalks for about 3 minutes. In a blender pulse the stalks with a ladle of stock.

In a heavy saucepan cook the onion in half the butter and the olive oil over a low heat for about 10 minutes until soft. Add the rice and cook gently, stirring, for 2 minutes to coat the rice with the oil. Start to add the stock, ladle by ladle, stirring constantly, allowing each ladleful to be absorbed before adding the next. Continue until the rice is al dente, usually about 20 minutes, add the stalk purée, vermouth, asparagus tips, the rest of the butter, and the Parmesan.

Stir to combine and season. Serve with Parmesan.

Risotto con ricotta e basilico
Risotto with ricotta and basil

For 6

1 quart Chicken Stock (see page 142)
coarse sea salt and freshly ground black pepper
3/4 cup fresh ricotta cheese
3 tablespoons olive oil
1 medium red onion, peeled and finely chopped
1 1/2 cups risotto rice
1/2 cup fresh basil leaves, finely chopped
1/2 cup freshly grated Parmesan

Heat the Chicken Stock, and check for seasoning.

Place the ricotta in a bowl and break up into small lumps with a fork.

Heat the oil in a large saucepan over a low heat and cook the onion for about 10 minutes until soft. Add the rice and turn to coat with oil and onion. The rice should not color, but become translucent. Start to add the hot seasoned stock, ladle by ladle, allowing each ladleful to be absorbed by the rice before adding the next. Continue cooking until the rice is al dente, usually about 20 minutes.

Lightly fold in the basil, ricotta, and Parmesan. Check for seasoning and serve immediately.

Risi e bisi

For 6

6 pounds fresh young peas in their pods
6 cups Chicken Stock (see page 142)
coarse sea salt and freshly ground black pepper
1/4 cup chopped fresh mint
2 tablespoons unsalted butter
3 tablespoons extra virgin olive oil
1 small red onion, peeled and finely chopped
1 1/2 cups risotto rice
1/4 cup chopped fresh flat-leaf parsley
1/2 cup freshly grated Parmesan

Choose the greenest and crispest peas. Shell them and keep about half of the pods. To prepare the selected pods for dissolving into the soup, pull the sides apart and peel away the thin membrane on the inside of each side. It will come away easily if you snap off the stalk and pull the membrane slowly down the length of the pod. Trim away the stringy edges.

To start the risotto-soup, heat the Chicken Stock to a slow boil and check for seasoning. Blanch half the peas and 3 tablespoons of the mint leaves in the boiling stock. Remove using a slotted spoon, and put in a food processor with a ladle of stock. Pulse-chop to a rough purée. Set aside.

Melt the butter and oil together in a heavy-bottomed saucepan. Add the onion and fry gently until the onion begins to color.

Add the rice and stir to coat each grain with onion, oil, and butter for 3-4 minutes. Add the remaining fresh peas and chopped mint, and then the prepared pods. Stir and fry for just a minute, then add the stock, ladle by ladle, as for a regular risotto. Stir all the time, keeping the mixture very wet.

Just before the rice is al dente, add the pea purée, and stir to heat through. Then add the parsley and half the Parmesan. Season, and sprinkle with the remaining Parmesan.

Risotto verde con pancetta
Green risotto with pancetta

For 6 To make the risotto even greener, add 3 ounces blanched and pulse-chopped peas to the spinach.

1 pound spinach, tough stalks removed
1 bunch fresh mint, leaves picked from the stalks
coarse sea salt and freshly ground black pepper
1 quart Chicken Stock (see page 142)
2 tablespoons unsalted butter
1 red onion, peeled and finely chopped
1/2 pound pancetta, cut into fine matchsticks
1 1/2 cups risotto rice
1/3 cup extra dry white vermouth
1/2 cup freshly grated Pecorino or Parmesan
freshly grated nutmeg

Wash the spinach thoroughly, then blanch with the mint in plenty of boiling salted water.

Drain the spinach and mint, cool, and chop finely. We use a food processor.

Heat the Chicken Stock and check for seasoning.

In a heavy-bottomed pan melt most of the butter and gently fry the chopped onion and pancetta together until the onion begins to turn golden and the pancetta becomes translucent. Add the rice and stir to coat each grain for 3-4 minutes. The rice should become translucent. Start to add the hot stock, ladle by ladle, constantly stirring, allowing each ladle to be absorbed by the rice before adding the next. Continue until the rice is al dente, usually about 20 minutes, then add the chopped spinach and mint, the remaining butter in small pieces, the vermouth, and half the Pecorino or Parmesan.

Combine well. Adjust the seasoning with salt, pepper, and nutmeg to taste. Serve with the remaining Pecorino or Parmesan.

Risotto verde alle erbe
Green risotto with herbs

For 6 This risotto is completely vegetarian.

2 pounds spinach, tough stalks removed

1 bunch fresh mint, leaves picked from the stalks

coarse sea salt and freshly ground black pepper

2 1/2 cups shelled peas

1 quart Vegetable Stock (see page 143)

2 tablespoons unsalted butter

2 small red onions, peeled and finely chopped

1/2 head celery, chopped (chop leaves too and set aside)

1 garlic clove, peeled and chopped

2 tablespoons chopped fresh thyme

1 1/2 cups risotto rice

1/3 cup extra dry white vermouth

1/2 cup freshly grated Parmesan

3 tablespoons each of chopped fresh marjoram and basil

1/4 cup cream

Wash the spinach thoroughly then blanch with the mint in plenty of boiling salted water. Drain well, keeping the water. Blanch the peas in the same water, then drain. Blend the spinach, peas, and mint to a rough purée in a food processor.

Heat the Vegetable Stock and check for seasoning.

In a heavy-bottomed saucepan, melt half the butter and gently fry the onion and celery until soft. Add the chopped garlic, celery leaves, and thyme, stir to combine, and cook for a few minutes before adding the rice. Stir to coat each grain for a few minutes. The rice should become translucent. Add the vermouth and cook, stirring constantly, until it is absorbed. Start to add the hot stock, ladle by ladle, constantly stirring, allowing each ladle to be absorbed by the rice before adding the next. Continue until the rice is al dente, usually about 20 minutes, then add the spinach and pea purée and the remainder of the butter.

Combine the grated Parmesan with the chopped herbs and the cream. Serve the risotto with the Parmesan and herb cream stirred in.

Risotto con funghi di bosco
Wild mushroom risotto

For 6 A good mixture of wild mushrooms is best (see below). Choose whatever you can get hold of, but you need at least a good 1 1/2 pounds in total to serve six.

1 1/2 pounds mixed wild mushrooms (fresh porcini, girolles, chanterelles gris, trompettes de mort)
2 ounces dried porcini, soaked for 30 minutes in hot water, drained, and roughly chopped (liquid strained and reserved)
1/4 cup olive oil
4-5 garlic cloves, peeled and finely chopped
coarse sea salt and freshly ground black pepper
2 cups Chicken Stock (see page 142)
2 tablespoons unsalted butter
1 red onion, peeled and finely chopped
1 1/2 cups risotto rice
1 cup freshly grated Parmesan
1 bunch fresh flat-leaf parsley, leaves picked from the stalks, finely chopped

Pick through the mushrooms, removing leaves and base of stems. Clean the fresh porcini and the girolles by brushing them lightly with a dry pastry brush. Submerge the chanterelles gris and trompettes de mort briefly in cold water and wash them vigorously. Immediately drain and dry in a salad spinner. Tear any larger mushrooms into smaller pieces.

In a large heavy saucepan heat 3 tablespoons of the olive oil until smoking. Add the mushrooms to the oil in small batches. Add half the chopped garlic after a minute or two. Season and fry for a couple of minutes more until cooked.

Heat the Chicken Stock and check for seasoning.

In a heavy-bottomed pan heat half the butter with the remaining olive oil. Add the chopped onion and cook on a gentle heat until the onion is soft.

Add the dried porcini to the pan with the remaining garlic. Cook for a minute. Add the rice and stir until each grain is coated. Start adding the stock, ladle by ladle, constantly stirring, allowing each ladleful to be absorbed by the rice before adding the next. Add some of the porcini liquid to the stock for flavor, and continue until the rice is cooked al dente, usually about 20 minutes. Add the cooked wild mushrooms, the remaining butter, the Parmesan, and chopped parsley. Serve immediately.

Risotto al rosmarino
Rosemary risotto

For 6

1 quart Chicken Stock (see page 142)

coarse sea salt and freshly ground black pepper

1 pound very ripe plum tomatoes

2 tablespoons unsalted butter

2 tablespoons olive oil

1 head celery, white tender parts only, finely chopped

1 small red onion, peeled and finely chopped

4 garlic cloves, peeled and finely chopped

2 branches very fresh rosemary, leaves picked from the stalks, finely chopped, plus 6
    small sprigs for serving

1 1/2 cups risotto rice

6 teaspoons mascarpone cheese

1 cup freshly grated Parmesan

Heat the Chicken Stock, and check for seasoning.

Blanch the tomatoes in boiling water for a minute, remove, and place in ice water. Skin and seed them into a sieve over a bowl to reserve the juices. Discard the seeds and skin. Chop the tomatoes finely.

In a heavy-bottomed pan heat the butter and olive oil. Add the celery and onion and cook on a low heat for 5 minutes; they should become soft and slightly colored. Add the garlic and chopped rosemary, cook for a minute, then add half of the tomato pulp. Stir to allow the tomato to reduce for 3-4 minutes before adding the rice. Stir the rice into the sauce to allow it to absorb the red of the tomato, cooking it for about 5 minutes. Start adding the hot stock ladle by ladle, alternating it with the reserved tomato liquid; stir constantly and allow each ladleful to be absorbed by the rice before adding the next. Add the remaining chopped tomato pulp about halfway through the cooking. Cook, stirring constantly, until the rice is al dente, usually about 20 minutes. Check for seasoning. Serve with a spoon of mascarpone, some Parmesan, and a sprig of rosemary.

Risotto con finocchio e vodka
Risotto with fennel and vodka

For 6

3 fennel bulbs, with their green tops

2 garlic cloves, peeled

1 1/2 small dried red chiles

1 1/2 teaspoons fennel seeds

coarse sea salt and freshly ground black pepper

1 cup vodka

juice of 1 1/2 lemons

1 quart Chicken Stock (see page 142)

2 tablespoons unsalted butter

2 tablespoons olive oil

1 small red onion, peeled and finely chopped

1 1/2 cups risotto rice

1/2 cup freshly grated Parmesan

Remove and discard the tough outer leaves of the fennel bulbs and finely chop the remainder of the bulbs. Chop the fennel tops and keep separately.

In a pestle and mortar crush the garlic, dried chile, and fennel seeds with 1 teaspoon salt.

In a bowl, mix the vodka, lemon juice, and chopped fennel tops to allow their flavors to combine.

Heat the Chicken Stock, and check for seasoning.

Melt half the butter and the olive oil in a saucepan, then add the chopped onion. Cook for a minute or two, keeping the heat low, then add the fennel seed paste from the mortar and let it cook briefly before adding the chopped fennel bulb. Let this cook slowly until soft. Add the rice and stir for a minute to coat each grain. Start to add the hot stock, ladle by ladle, stirring continuously, and allowing each ladleful to be absorbed by the rice before adding the next. Continue until the rice is al dente, usually about 20 minutes, then stir in the remaining butter and the vodka, fennel tops, and lemon juice mixture. Sprinkle with Parmesan.

Risotto con polpa di granchio
Crab risotto

For 6

3 tablespoons olive oil
1 small red onion, peeled and finely chopped
2 small fennel bulbs, finely chopped (keep the leaves, chop, and set aside)
3 garlic cloves, peeled and chopped
10 fennel seeds, crushed
2 small dried red chiles, crumbled
1 1/2 cups risotto rice
1 28-ounce can peeled plum tomatoes, drained of their juices
6 cups Fish Stock (see page 142)
coarse sea salt and freshly ground black pepper
1/3 cup Italian Chardonnay
5-pound live crab boiled and cooled
juice of 2 lemons
1 bunch fresh flat-leaf parsley, roughly chopped
extra virgin olive oil

Heat the oil in a heavy-bottomed saucepan. Add the onion and fennel and fry together, stirring, over a low heat until soft and beginning to color. Add the garlic and cook briefly, then add the fennel seeds and chile. Stir, and as soon as the garlic turns in color, add the rice and stir to coat. Add the drained tomatoes and break them up into the rice to allow the tomato to be absorbed before you start to add the stock. You can raise the temperature a little, but always stir to prevent sticking.

Heat the Fish Stock, and check for seasoning.

Add the Chardonnay to the rice and cook, stirring constantly, for a minute or until the wine too is absorbed. Reduce the heat and over a low flame, gently stirring, add the hot Fish Stock, ladle by ladle, constantly stirring, allowing each ladle to be absorbed by the rice before adding the next. Continue until the rice is al dente, usually about 20 minutes.

Stir in first the crabmeat with the lemon juice, then the parsley and fennel leaves, folding in gently, just sufficiently for the crabmeat to heat through. Check for seasoning, and serve the risotto with some extra virgin olive oil on the top.

Risotto con trevisano e pancetta
Treviso radicchio and pancetta risotto

For 6 True Italian treviso radicchio has long pointed leaves and is sold on the stalk, which is also delicious.

1 quart Chicken Stock (see page 142)
coarse sea salt and freshly ground black pepper
5 heads Treviso raddicchio
1 red onion, peeled and finely chopped
2 celery stalks, finely chopped
4 ounces pancetta, cut into fine matchsticks
6 tablespoons unsalted butter
1 garlic clove, peeled and crushed
1 1/2 cups risotto rice
2/3 cup red wine
1/2 cup freshly grated Parmesan

Heat the Chicken Stock, and check for seasoning.

Trim the radicchio, and cut the leaves from the white ribs. Chop both red and white, and keep separate.

Fry the onion, celery, and pancetta in 2 tablespoons of the butter until the onion and celery are light gold and soft, and the pancetta has become translucent. Add the garlic and the white parts of the radicchio, stir, and cook for 2 minutes. Add the rice and turn to coat the rice, combining the flavors. Pour in the wine, allow it to reduce and color the rice, then start to add the hot seasoned stock, ladle by ladle. Allow each ladleful to be absorbed by the rice before adding the next. Continue in this way until the rice is al dente, usually about 20 minutes.

In a separate saucepan heat 4 tablespoons of the remaining butter. Add the red part of the radicchio and cook for a minute. Stir into the finished risotto, then add the remaining butter and the Parmesan.

Risotto con tartufi bianchi
White truffle risotto

For 6

1 quart Chicken Stock (see page 142)

coarse sea salt and freshly ground black pepper

4 tablespoons unsalted butter

1 small red onion, peeled and finely chopped

1 head celery, white tender part only, finely chopped

1 1/2 cups risotto rice

6 tablespoons vermouth

2/3 cup cream

1/2 teaspoon freshly grated nutmeg

3/4 cup freshly grated Parmesan

5-6 ounces white truffles, carefully brushed clean

Heat the Chicken Stock, and check for seasoning.

Melt half the butter in a heavy-bottomed saucepan, and gently fry the onion and celery until soft and beginning to brown. Add the rice and stir to combine the rice with the vegetables and coat it with butter. The rice should become opaque. Start to add the hot stock, ladle by ladle, stirring all the time, allowing the rice to absorb each ladleful before adding the next. Add the vermouth and cream just before the rice is cooked. Season with salt, pepper, and a few gratings of nutmeg. Finally stir in the remaining butter and half the Parmesan.

Serve on warm plates with the remaining Parmesan, and generously shave the truffles equally over each portion.

Risotto al limone con basilico
Lemon risotto with basil

For 6

1 quart Chicken Stock (see page 142)
coarse sea salt and freshly ground black pepper
4 tablespoons unsalted butter
1 red onion, peeled and finely chopped
1 head celery, white parts only, chopped, plus leaves
1 garlic clove, peeled and chopped
1 1/2 cups risotto rice
2/3 cup dry vermouth
6 tablespoons roughly chopped fresh basil
juice and zest of 4 large washed lemons
1/2 cup freshly grated Parmesan
5 tablespoons mascarpone cheese

Heat the Chicken Stock, and check for seasoning.

Melt half the butter in a heavy-bottomed saucepan. Gently fry the onion and celery stalk until soft. Add the garlic and celery leaves, stir to combine, then add the rice. Stir the rice to coat then add the vermouth. Allow it to bubble and reduce, then add the hot stock ladle by ladle over a gentle heat. Stir constantly and allow each ladleful to be absorbed before adding another.

When the rice is al dente, usually after about 20 minutes, stir in most of the basil, the lemon juice and zest, half the Parmesan, and the mascarpone. Stir once; the texture should be creamy. Serve with a few basil leaves and the remaining Parmesan.

Soup
Stoc

os
ks
5

Ribollita d'estiva   Acquacotta di primavera   Acquace

Zuppa di fave fresche   Zuppa di cannellini e cicoria   Z

Brodo di finocchio e ricotta   Brodo di pesce   Brodo di p

ca   Zuppa di castagne, zucca, e farro   Zuppa lombarda
ppa di rucola e patate   Zuppa di baccalà   Zuppa di farro
lo   Brodo di verdura   Zuppa di orzo

Ribollita d'estiva
Summer ribollita

For 8

2 1/4 cups fresh borlotti (or cannellini) beans, shelled weight, cooked (see page 346)

extra virgin olive oil

4 young onions, red or white, peeled and chopped

1 head celery, plus leaves, stalks chopped

1 head fresh garlic, peeled and sliced

1 pound Swiss chard stalks and leaves, stalks sliced into large matchsticks

1 bunch fresh basil, leaves picked from the stalks

1 bunch fresh mint, leaves picked from the stalks

1 bunch fresh marjoram, leaves picked from the stalks

1 bunch fresh flat-leaf parsley, leaves picked from the stalks

4 pounds fresh ripe plum tomatoes, skinned, seeded, and chopped

coarse sea salt and freshly ground black pepper

1 bunch fresh borage (optional)

10 ounces fresh spinach, tough stalks removed

2 loaves ciabatta bread, stale if possible, crusts removed

1 fresh red chile

In a large heavy pan heat 1/4 cup of olive oil, then add the onion and celery stalks. Stir and cook gently until they soften and brown. Add the garlic and chard stalks and continue to cook. When the garlic begins to color, add half the basil, mint, marjoram, parsley, and celery leaves. Gently fry and stir together to combine the herbs, then add the chopped tomatoes. Season and simmer for 30 minutes: the tomatoes should reduce with the vegetables.

Separately, in another large saucepan full of boiling water with plenty of salt, blanch the borage and chard leaves and then the spinach. Drain, keeping the blanching water, and roughly chop. Add the leaves to the vegetable and tomato mixture along with the cooked beans. Tear up the bread into 1-2-in lengths and add to the soup. Pour over some of the blanching water to moisten the bread, and stir in the remaining herbs. Check for seasoning, then add salt and pepper to taste and 1/4 cup olive oil. The consistency should be very thick.

Get rid of the seeds and fibers from the inside of the red chile by cutting it in half and scraping with a teaspoon. Chop the chile roughly, then place in a small bowl and add 2 tablespoons extra virgin olive oil. To serve, dribble this chile sauce over each bowl of soup when serving.

Acquacotta di primavera
Spring acquacotta

For 6

1/2 pound asparagus
6 small artichoke hearts (see page 172)
zest and juice of 1 lemon
1 pound Swiss chard
1 1/4 cups shelled fresh peas
1 1/4 cups shelled fresh young fava beans
3 tablespoons olive oil
3 garlic cloves, peeled and finely chopped
coarse sea salt and freshly ground black pepper
2 tablespoons each of chopped fresh parsley, basil, and thyme
6 crostini (see page 290)

Cut off and discard the hard part of the asparagus stalks. Slice each artichoke heart into four and put in a bowl of water with the lemon juice. Separate the stalks from the leaves of the chard. Cut the stalks into 1/4-in pieces, and roughly chop the leaves.

In a saucepan, heat the oil and fry the garlic until golden. Add the artichokes. After 2 minutes add the chard stalks and cook together until soft and beginning to color.

Add half the peas, fava beans, and chard leaves, season, and just cover with boiling water. Cook over a moderate heat for 20 minutes. Add the remaining vegetables and cook for a further 5 minutes. Add the lemon zest and the herbs at the last moment and serve with a crostini in each soup bowl.

Acquacotta

For 6-8

3 ounces dried porcini
2 red onions, peeled
1 head celery
2 carrots, peeled
4 garlic cloves, peeled
3 tablespoons olive oil
1 small bunch fresh thyme
1/2 bunch fresh parsley
2 small dried red chiles, crumbled
2 1/2 28-ounce cans peeled plum tomatoes, plus their juices
coarse sea salt and freshly ground black pepper
6 crostini (see page 290)
extra virgin olive oil
1/2 cup freshly grated Parmesan

Place the porcini in a bowl and pour boiling water over them. Leave for 15 minutes.

Roughly chop the onions. Remove and discard the tough outer stalks from the celery, and cut the tender heart and green leaves into small pieces. Cut the carrots roughly into 1/2-in slices. Slice the garlic finely.

Heat the oil in a large heavy-bottomed saucepan and gently fry the onion with the celery and carrot until soft and lightly colored. Add the thyme, garlic, parsley, and chile, and continue to fry, stirring to combine the flavors. The longer you cook at this stage, the better the flavor of the soup will be.

Drain the porcini, keeping the soaking liquid, and add the porcini to the onion and celery. Fry together for a few minutes, then add the tomatoes (but not the juice), one by one. Break them up with a spoon and stir into the onion mixture. When the tomatoes have begun to thicken – this will take about 30-45 minutes – add a little of the tomato juice and the strained reserved porcini water. Stir and cook togeth gently for about another 30 minutes. Your soup should be thick. Season with salt a pepper.

Place a crostini in each soup bowl, then ladle in the soup. Drizzle with extra virg olive oil and sprinkle with Parmesan.

Zuppa di castagne, zucca, e farro
Chestnut, pumpkin, and farro soup

For 6

2 pounds fresh chestnuts, boiled, peeled, and roughly chopped

2 1/4 pounds pumpkin flesh, roasted and roughly chopped (see page 158)

4 ounces farro, soaked in cold water for 1 1/2 hours

6 tablespoons olive oil

1 red onion, peeled and finely chopped

1 head celery, roughly chopped

4 ounces pancetta, finely diced

5 garlic cloves, peeled and chopped

2 tablespoons fresh rosemary, chopped

2 dried red chiles, crumbled

1 quart Chicken Stock (see page 142)

coarse sea salt and freshly ground black pepper

extra virgin olive oil

Drain the farro, then put in a pan, cover with cold water, and bring to the boil. Cook until the faro expands and is al dente, about 20 minutes.

Meanwhile, in a heavy saucepan large enough to hold the soup, heat 3 tablespoons of the olive oil. Add the onion and celery, fry gently to soften, then add the pancetta, garlic, chopped rosemary, and chile. Allow this to cook on a low heat until the pancetta and garlic begin to color, then add the chestnuts. Let them absorb the pancetta flavors, about 5 minutes, then add the pumpkin. Cook this for a further 5 minutes, then add the warmed Chicken Stock. Finally add the cooked farro. Heat through, check for seasoning, then serve, drizzled with extra virgin olive oil.

Zuppa lombarda
Broth with cannellini beans and ciabatta

For 6 It is essential to make the broth for this soup yourself with the best organic chicken you can find.

2 quarts Chicken Stock (see page 142)
1 cup dried cannellini beans, soaked overnight and cooked (see page 346)
coarse sea salt and freshly ground black pepper
12 crostini, sliced very thinly (see page 290)
extra virgin olive oil

Heat the cooked cannellini beans, then take out 1 1/4 cups of them, plus their cooking water, and purée to a cream in the food processor. Return to the whole beans.

Skim off any chicken fat from the surface of the broth. Season the broth to taste with salt and pepper. It should be sweet and clear. Heat.

Place 2 crostini in each soup bowl, then pour over the hot broth. Top with 1/4 cup of cooked cannellini beans and the liquid they cooked in. Serve drizzled with extra virgin olive oil.

Zuppa di fave fresche
Fresh fava bean soup

For 6

6 pounds very young fava beans, shelled

3 pounds very young peas, shelled

2 tablespoons olive oil

1 red onion, peeled and finely sliced

2 medium potatoes, peeled and sliced

1 bunch fresh mint, leaves removed from the stalks (retain the stalks)

water or Chicken Stock (see page 142)

coarse sea salt and freshly ground black pepper

3 tablespoons chopped fresh mint

Heat the olive oil in a heavy-bottomed pan, and gently fry the onion until soft and translucent. Add the peas and potatoes, and cook, stirring, for 5 minutes, then add a handful of the mint. Pour in enough stock or water to cover, and simmer for 15 minutes. Add half the fava beans after 5 minutes.

In a separate pan boil 9 cups of water. Add the mint stalks and the remaining beans. Cook, covered, for 2-3 minutes. Drain, and discard the stalks.

Put a ladle of the soup mixture in the food processor with a ladle of blanched fava beans, and pulse-chop. Keep to one side. Pulse-chop the remainder of the soup with the rest of the mint leaves. Return to the pan. Add the remaining whole fava beans and the puréed fava beans, and season the soup well with salt and pepper.

Reheat gently and serve with the chopped fresh mint. The soup should be very thick with a combination of whole young fava beans and a rough purée.

Zuppa di cannellini e cicoria
Cannellini bean and bitter cicoria soup

For 6 Bitter cicoria is a cultivated dandelion leaf grown in Italy.

1 1/4 cups dried cannellini beans, soaked and cooked (see page 346)
2 pounds cicoria or escarole
coarse sea salt and freshly ground black pepper
extra virgin olive oil
2 garlic cloves, peeled and chopped
1 dried red chile, crumbled

Cook the cannellini beans as described on page 346, then leave to rest in their cooking water.

Prepare the cicoria. Strip the green from the thick stems where they are tough and stringy and cut into pieces about 3/4 in in length. Blanch in a large saucepan of boiling salted water. Remove and refresh under cold water, then drain well and chop coarsely.

Heat 2 tablespoons olive oil in a large pan and cook the garlic lightly until soft, then add the cicoria pieces. Cook for a minute, then add salt, pepper, and the chile.

Drain the cannellini beans, reserving their liquid, and stir into the cicoria mixture. Put three-quarters of this into a food processor with a little of the bean liquid, and briefly pulse. If it is too thick to mix, add more liquid. Return the mixture to the pan with the whole beans, and mix together. Season with salt, pepper, and more chile according to taste. Add more liquid if necessary, but this is meant to be a very thick soup.

Serve with a generous amount of extra virgin olive oil.

Zuppa di rucola e patate
Arugula and potato soup

For 6

2 pounds Yukon Gold potatoes, peeled and cut into 1/2-in dice

2 pounds arugula, tough stalks removed, leaves roughly chopped

6 cups Chicken Stock (see page 142), well seasoned

coarse sea salt and freshly ground black pepper

olive oil

3 garlic cloves, peeled and chopped

2 dried red chiles, crumbled

3 tablespoons roughly chopped fresh parsley

6 crostini (see page 290)

freshly grated Parmesan

1 fresh red chile, seeded, chopped, and marinated in 2 tablespoons olive oil

Heat the Chicken Stock and check it for seasoning.

In a large heavy-bottomed saucepan, heat 3 tablespoons olive oil and gently fry the garlic until golden. Add the chile and potatoes and stir-fry for a few minutes. Add the parsley and half the arugula and cook for just a few seconds. Add about 3 ladlefuls of the hot stock. Simmer on a medium heat, stirring quite frequently, for about 20 minutes. The potatoes should break up into the stock, but small pieces will remain. Put the remainder of the stock into a blender or food processor and add most of the rest of the arugula. Pulse together, then stir this liquid into the soup. Check for seasoning.

Place a crostini in each bowl, then add a tablespoon of fresh arugula and a tablespoon of Parmesan. Ladle over the hot soup. Serve with a teaspoon of chile oil.

Zuppa di baccalà
Salt cod soup

For 6

2 pounds salt cod (baccalà), soaked (see page 212)

3 tablespoons olive oil

1 medium red onion, peeled and finely sliced

1/2 head celery, plus leaves, stalks finely sliced

3 garlic cloves, peeled and finely sliced

2 tablespoons chopped fresh thyme

3 bay leaves

1 teaspoon fennel seeds, crushed

2 small dried red chiles, crumbled

6 ripe plum tomatoes, skinned, seeded, and chopped

2/3 cup dry white wine

6 small potatoes, peeled and cut into quarters

freshly ground black pepper

1/4 cup chopped fresh flat-leaf parsley

6 crostini (see page 290)

2 fresh red chiles, seeded and chopped

extra virgin olive oil

Cut the salt cod into 4-in pieces.

Heat the olive oil in a heavy-bottomed pan and fry the onion for a minute until softened, then add the celery stalks, leaves, and garlic, and cook until slightly colored. Now add the thyme, bay leaves, crushed fennel seeds, and dried chile. Stir for a second just to combine, then add the tomatoes. Push the tomatoes into the onion mixture to break up any pieces, and stir. As soon as the tomatoes become sticky, add the wine, potatoes, and enough water to cover. Cook, stirring frequently, until the potatoes are al dente.

Add the cod, lower the heat, and simmer, covered, for 15-20 minutes. The cod should be tender and just beginning to break up. Add pepper to taste and most of the parsley.

Place one crostini in each soup bowl, pour over the broth and pieces of cod, and sprinkle with the remainder of the parsley and a little fresh chile. Serve drizzled with extra virgin olive oil.

Zuppa di farro
Soup of farro, borlotti, cannellini, and chickpeas
For 6

1 cup farro, soaked in salted water for 2 hours

1/2 cup dried borlotti beans, cooked (see page 346), cooking liquid retained

1/2 cup cannellini beans, cooked (see page 346), cooking liquid retained

1/2 cup chickpeas, cooked (see page 214)

1/4 cup olive oil

3 garlic cloves, peeled and coarsely sliced

1 28-ounce can peeled plum tomatoes

3 sprigs fresh rosemary, chopped

coarse sea salt and freshly ground black pepper

6 crostini (see page 290)

extra virgin olive oil

Drain the farro. Put in a saucepan, cover, and bring to the boil. Reduce the heat and simmer for 45 minutes or until al dente.

Heat 1 tablespoon of the oil in a heavy-bottomed pan, and fry 1 garlic clove until soft. Add the tomatoes and their juices, and cook, stirring, over a moderate heat for half an hour. Season and set aside.

Heat the remaining olive oil in a large pan, and add the remaining garlic and rosemary. When the garlic begins to color, add the tomato sauce and stir. Add the beans and their cooking liquid and the drained chickpeas, bring to a boil, and add the farro. Cook for a further 15 minutes then season.

Place a crostini in each soup bowl and ladle the soup over. Drizzle with olive oil.

Brodo di finochio e ricotta
Sardinian wild fennel soup

For 6

4 medium fennel bulbs, with leaves
6 cups Chicken Stock (see page 142)
coarse sea salt and freshly ground black pepper
6 crostini (see page 290)
1 cup ricotta cheese
extra virgin olive oil
1/2 cup freshly grated Parmesan

Slice the fine leaves from the top of the fennel and set aside. Remove the tough or bruised outside layer of the fennel and trim the base. With the base on the board, stand the fennel up, and slice down, making pieces about 1/2 in thick.

Bring the Chicken Stock to the boil and add the fennel pieces. Cook until very tender, about 20 minutes. Add the fennel leaves and season with salt and pepper.

Place a crostini in each soup bowl. Cut the ricotta into thin slices and place on top of the crostini. Spoon over the cooked fennel pieces, then ladle in some of the stock. Drizzle olive oil over each bowl then sprinkle with the Parmesan.

Brodo di pesce
Fish stock

Makes 6 cups This is the stock to use for
the risotto on page 112.

heads and bones of 1-2 large turbot,
    halibut, or monkfish
1 piece sea bass or head
a handful each of fennel and parsley stalks
1 whole head garlic
1/2 head celery with leaves
2 large plum tomatoes
1/2 tablespoon each of fennel seeds,
    coriander seeds, and white peppercorns
2 bay leaves
2 dried red chiles
2/3 dry white wine
7-8 cups cold water
coarse sea salt

Put all the ingredients, apart from the
salt, into a large pan and bring to the
boil, skimming off any scum if
necessary. Lower the heat and simmer
very gently for about 30 minutes. Strain
and use immediately, seasoning to
taste with salt.

Brodo di pollo
Chicken stock

Makes 9 cups In a perfect world – i.e. in
Bologna for instance – the stock would include a
veal bone, a beef shin, and a piece of pancetta.

3 1/4-4 1/2-pound free-range chicken, all
    fatty parts removed
1 head celery, white parts only, washed
2 large carrots, scrubbed
1 small red onion, peeled
2 tomatoes
1 head garlic, unpeeled
5 bay leaves
3 sprigs fresh thyme
1 teaspoon black peppercorns
3 quarts cold water
coarse sea salt

Put the chicken and the rest of the
ingredients, apart from the salt, into a
large saucepan, and bring gently to the
boil. Turn the heat down and skim, then
gently simmer for about 1 hour. Remove
the chicken and strain out the
vegetables and herbs. Season the broth
to taste with salt.

Brodo di verdura
Vegetable stock

Makes 9 cups

2 tablespoons olive oil

2 small red onions, peeled and roughly
    sliced

4 carrots, washed and halved

1 head celery, stalks and leaves, cut
    lengthways into four

4 leeks, tough green tops removed, halved

2 fennel bulbs, each cut into four

2 dried red chiles

4 garlic cloves, peeled

1 bunch fresh thyme

1 bunch flat-leaf parsley, leaves picked from
the stalks (retain both)

9 cups water

4 bay leaves

2 tablespoons white or black peppercorns

juice of 1 lemon

coarse sea salt

Heat the oil in a large heavy-bottomed saucepan, then gently fry the onion until soft. Add the carrot, celery, leek, and fennel, and fry, stirring, until lightly browned. Add the chile, garlic, thyme, and parsley leaves, stir to combine, and continue to cook. Add the water, parsley stalks, bay leaves, and peppercorns, and bring to the boil. Lower the heat and simmer gently for about 1 hour before straining. Add the lemon juice and adjust the seasoning.

Zuppa di orzo
Barley soup

For 6

1 1/2 cups barley, soaked in hot water for 45 minutes

1/4 cup olive oil

1 head celery, tender stalks and young leaves separated and roughly chopped

1 red onion, peeled and chopped

1 fennel bulb, chopped, green herb parts chopped separately

3 leeks, white parts no thicker than your thumb, chopped

2 garlic cloves, peeled and finely chopped

2 small dried red chiles, crumbled

2 tablespoons each chopped fresh flat-leaf parsley and mint

4 fresh ripe tomatoes, peeled, seeded, and chopped

9 cups Chicken Stock (see page 142)

coarse sea salt and freshly ground black pepper

extra virgin olive oil (peppery new season estate-bottled is the best)

Heat the oil in a heavy saucepan then add the celery and onion and cook together until they begin to soften. Add the fennel bulb and leek and fry, stirring, until they begin to caramelize, about 15 minutes. Add the garlic and chile, then, after 1 minute, the herbs, celery leaves, and tomatoes. Stir to combine and slightly reduce, then add half the barley. Allow to absorb the flavors, then add half the Chicken Stock. Reduce the heat and cook until the barley is tender, about 30-40 minutes.

Cook the remaining barley in the rest of the stock for 30-40 minutes. Purée in a food processor and add to the soup. Season and serve with extra virgin olive oil. This soup should be thick and creamy.

Wood-ı
Vegeta

oasted
bles

6

Zucchini al forno   Asparagi al forno   Pomidorini al
Barbe rosse in cartoccio   Barbe rosse intere al forno
Sedano rapa al forno   Trevisano con pancetta e rosma
freschi al forno   Carciofi in cartoccio con timo   Biet
con parmigiano   Patate e acciughe al forno

Zucchini al forno
Wood-roasted zucchini

For 6

18 small zucchini, trimmed and cut in half lengthways
3 garlic cloves, peeled and roughly chopped
coarse sea salt and freshly ground black pepper
4 teaspoons coriander seeds
olive oil
1 bunch fresh thyme, leaves picked from the stalks

Preheat the oven to 425° F.

Pound the garlic, a little salt, and the coriander seeds together until crushed.

Arrange the zucchini cut side up in an oiled roasting pan. Sprinkle the garlic mixture and thyme leaves loosely all over. Lightly drizzle with olive oil, and season well.

Roast the zucchini in the preheated oven for about 15 minutes until golden and cooked through.

Asparagi al forno
Wood-roasted asparagus

For 6

3 pounds asparagus
olive oil
1 bunch fresh basil, leaves picked from their stalks, roughly chopped
coarse sea salt and freshly ground black pepper
1 garlic clove, peeled and finely chopped
1/2 cup pitted Niçoise olives

Preheat the oven to 425° F.

Trim the asparagus of any woody stalks by gently flexing the base of the stem until it snaps. Discard the woody ends, and wash the green stalks and tips. Dry well and place in a mixing bowl. Toss with enough olive oil to lightly coat each stalk. Add the basil, salt, pepper, and garlic, and gently mix.

Arrange in an oiled roasting pan and season again. Add the olives.

Roast in the preheated oven for about 10 minutes or until the stalks are wilted and light gold in color.

Pomidorini al forno
Wood-roasted cherry vine tomatoes

For 6

3 pounds cherry tomatoes, on the vine, in about 10 small clusters
1/4 cup olive oil
1 bunch fresh thyme in small sprigs
3 garlic cloves, peeled and thinly sliced
coarse sea salt and freshly ground black pepper

Preheat the oven to 400° F. Place the tomatoes in an oiled roasting pan. Scatter with the thyme and garlic. Drizzle with oil, and season. Roast for 20 minutes.

Melanzane al forno
Wood-roasted eggplant

For 6

3 eggplants, sliced into rounds about 3/4 in thick
olive oil
2 tablespoons dried oregano
2 garlic cloves, peeled and finely chopped
coarse sea salt and freshly ground black pepper

Preheat the oven to 425° F. Lightly brush both sides of the eggplant slices with oil and place flat in a baking dish. Scatter with half the oregano and garlic and season. Bake for about 15 minutes. Turn over, sprinkle with the remaining oregano and garlic and more salt and pepper, and bake for another 5-10 minutes.

Cipolle rosse ripiene di timo
Baked red onions with thyme

For 6

12 small red onions, skins left on

4 garlic cloves, peeled and thinly sliced

1 bunch fresh thyme, leaves of 2 sprigs picked from the stalks

4 tablespoons unsalted butter, softened

coarse sea salt and freshly ground black pepper

2/3 cup balsamic vinegar

2/3 cup red wine

Preheat the oven to 350° F.

Trim the base of each onion, so that they can stand. Cut a deep cross in from the top, about halfway down the height of the onion. Stand the onions in a baking dish and place a couple of slivers of garlic and a small sprig of the thyme in the incisions. Mix the butter with the remaining thyme leaves, salt, and pepper, and put a teaspoonful on top of each onion. Drizzle the balsamic vinegar and red wine over the onions and season again. Cover with foil and bake in the preheated oven for about 40 minutes or until the onions have softened.

Remove the foil and reduce the oven temperature to 300° F, and continue to cook for another hour, basting frequently. To prevent the balsamic juices from drying up and burning, add 1 1/3 cups or so of water, or more red wine. Alternatively the temperature can be reduced to 250° F, and the onions can be roasted for longer. The onions are ready when they are soft and caramelized.

Barbe rosse in cartoccio
Baby beets baked in foil

For 6

18 small summer beets
6 tablespoons extra virgin olive oil
coarse sea salt and freshly ground black pepper
3 garlic cloves, peeled and thinly sliced
1 large bunch fresh thyme, leaves picked from the stalks
lemon juice from 2 lemons

Preheat the oven to 425° F.

Prepare the beets as in the recipe on the next page, but cutting the leaves off 2 in from the bulbs.

Cut foil into 7 x 5-in squares, or squares large enough to individually wrap each beet. Brush one side of the foil with olive oil. Scatter with salt and pepper, a few slices of garlic, and some thyme leaves. Place the beets on top and wrap carefully.

Place the parcels on a baking sheet and bake in the preheated oven for 45 minutes. Test by inserting the point of a knife; they should be soft.

Serve drizzled with extra virgin oil and lemon juice.

Barbe rosse intere al forno
Whole wood-roasted beets

For 6 Buy small beets roughly the size of golf balls with their leaves on and root tail intact.

18 small summer beets
1 bunch fresh thyme
4 garlic cloves, peeled and finely chopped
6 tablespoons extra virgin olive oil
3 tablespoons vinegar (balsamic or herb wine vinegar)
juice of 1 lemon
coarse sea salt
1 tablespoon freshly ground black pepper

Preheat the oven to 425° F.

Remove the beet leaves 1 1/4 in from the bulb, and put to one side (use them in the recipes on pages 42 and 60). Keep the root tail of the beets intact. Wash the beets thoroughly, dry, then put in a bowl.

Pull the leaves from the majority of the thyme stalks. Keep a few stalks whole.

Mix the garlic and thyme leaves and stalks with the olive oil, vinegar, and lemon juice, add the seasonings, and then pour over the beets. Turn over and over in the marinade, and then place in a baking dish. Bake for 20 minutes. Turn the beets over then bake for a further 20 minutes or until cooked.

Serve warm with other wood-roasted vegetables or cold with ricotta (see page 42).

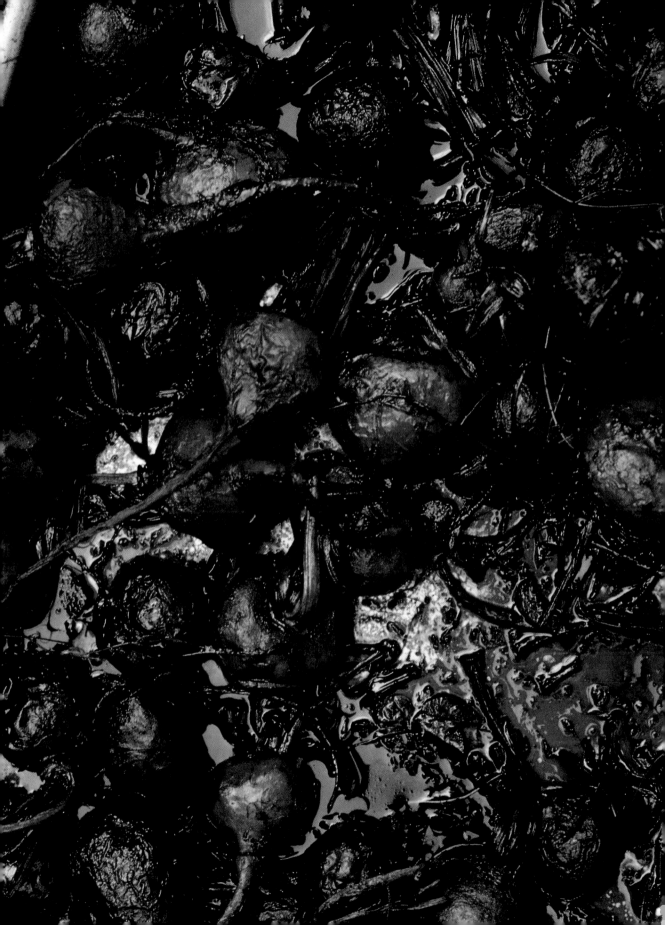

Carote intere al forno
Wood-roasted whole organic carrots

For 6

12 medium to large organic carrots, scrubbed and trimmed
2 tablespoons thyme leaves
2 garlic cloves, peeled
coarse sea salt and freshly ground black pepper
6 tablespoons olive oil
3 tablespoons herb wine vinegar (Volpaia "Erbe")

Preheat oven to 425° F. Pound together the thyme, garlic, salt, and pepper. Add the oil and vinegar. Pour over the carrots in a baking dish and toss. Roast for 35-40 minutes, turning after 20 minutes.

Zucca al forno
Wood-roasted pumpkin

For 6

1 small pumpkin, about 2 1/2 pounds, peeled, cut into wedges 3/4 in thick
1/2 cup olive oil
3 garlic cloves, peeled and finely chopped
1 small dried red chile, crumbled
1 bunch fresh thyme, leaves picked from the stalks
coarse sea salt and freshly ground black pepper

Preheat the oven to 400° F. Put the pumpkin pieces in a bowl with the other ingredients. Mix thoroughly to coat. Put in an oiled baking dish and roast for about an hour.

Topinambur al forno
Wood-roasted jerusalem artichokes

For 6 Roast sweet potatoes in the same way.

20 Jerusalem artichokes, peeled
6 tablespoons olive oil
1 small bunch fresh thyme, leaves picked from the stalks
3 garlic cloves, peeled and finely chopped
coarse sea salt and freshly ground black pepper

Preheat the oven to 425° F. Put the artichokes in a bowl with the other ingredients. Mix thoroughly. Place in an oiled baking dish and roast for about 25 minutes.

Sedano rapa al forno
Wood-roasted celery root

For 6

2 celery roots, about 1 pound each, peeled and cut into wedges 3/4 in thick
1 small bunch fresh thyme, leaves picked from the stalks
6 tablespoons olive oil
1 head garlic, separated into cloves, peeled and chopped
coarse sea salt and freshly ground black pepper

Preheat the oven to 425° F. Put the celery root in a bowl with the other ingredients. Mix thoroughly. Place in an oiled baking dish and cover loosely with foil. Bake for 10 minutes. Remove the foil, turn the pieces over, and roast for 20 minutes.

Trevisano con pancetta e rosmarino
Baked Treviso radicchio wrapped in pancetta

For 6

6 heads Treviso radicchio
24 small sprigs fresh rosemary
4 garlic cloves, peeled and sliced
coarse sea salt and freshly ground black pepper
24 thin slices pancetta, about 7 ounces
extra virgin olive oil

Preheat the oven to 400° F.

Prepare the radicchio by cutting each head into quarters lengthways so the leaves stay attached to the stem. Tuck a sprig of rosemary and a couple of garlic slices into each radicchio quarter, on the cut side, and season with salt and pepper. Wrap a piece of pancetta around each quarter of radicchio, tucking it in to prevent it falling off.

Place the wrapped radicchio pieces in a lightly oiled baking dish, drizzle with olive oil, and bake in the preheated oven until the radicchio stem is tender and the pancetta is crisp, about 10-15 minutes.

Porcini al forno
Wood-roasted whole porcini

For 6

6 large whole fresh porcini or portobello mushrooms, stems attached
12 large sprigs fresh thyme
18 thin slices smoked pancetta
3 garlic cloves, peeled and finely sliced
coarse sea salt and freshly ground black pepper
extra virgin olive oil
3 lemons
a handful of arugula

Preheat the oven to 450° F.

With a soft dry brush, clean each mushroom carefully. With a sharp knife make two cuts up the length of the stalk, dividing it equally into three parts, making sure it does not become separated from its cap. In each cut place a sprig of thyme, a slice of pancetta, and a few slices of garlic. Season generously, then wind a slice of pancetta round each stem to hold in the stuffing.

Heat a suitable roasting pan until hot, then add 1/4 cup olive oil. Place the porcini in the oil and put in the oven to bake. They take from 5-15 minutes according to the size and thickness of the cap. When ready, the cap will have browned and shrunk, the stem will have colored, and the pancetta will be cooked.

Remove the pan from the oven, and squeeze the juice of 1/2 lemon over each porcini. Serve with the arugula dressed with oil and extra lemon juice.

Cannellini secchi al forno
Baked dried cannellini beans

For 6

1 1/4 cups dried cannellini beans
1 head garlic
a handful of fresh sage leaves
6 tablespoons extra virgin olive oil
coarse sea salt and freshly ground black pepper

Soak the beans overnight in a generous amount of water.

Preheat the oven to 400° F.

Drain the beans well and place them in a baking dish. Add the garlic, sage, and enough water to come three-quarters up the sides of the baking dish. Pour in the olive oil to cover the beans. Cover the dish with foil and make a small hole in the center with the point of a knife to allow steam to escape.

Place the casserole in the preheated oven and cook until the beans are very tender, about 45 minutes – although the cooking time will vary according to the quality of the beans. The liquid will evaporate, and the beans will become very tender. Season generously with salt and black pepper.

Borlotti freschi al forno
Baked fresh borlotti beans

For 6 You can cook fresh or dried borlotti beans in this way. The fresh will obviously take less time.

4 pounds fresh borlotti beans, shelled
3 large tomatoes
1 whole garlic clove with its skin
1 bunch fresh sage
1/2 cup extra virgin olive oil
coarse sea salt and freshly ground black pepper

Preheat the oven to 400° F.

Choose an ovenproof saucepan or casserole. The size of the pan is important; the beans should fill it to halfway up the sides. Put in the beans, whole tomatoes, garlic, and sage, and pour in cold water just to come within 1/4 in of the top of the beans. Pour in the olive oil, or enough to cover the surface of the beans by about 1/2 in. Seal tightly with foil, and make a hole in the middle with the point of a knife to allow steam to escape.

Place the beans in the preheated oven and bake for 3/4-1 hour. The water evaporates during cooking, and the beans will soak up the olive oil, becoming creamy and soft. Season generously with salt and black pepper.

If you have a wood oven, the beans can be cooked in the cooler oven overnight.

When serving, add a little green, fruity extra virgin olive oil.

Carciofi in cartoccio con timo
Artichokes baked in foil with thyme

For 6

12 small young artichokes with stems attached
1/2 lemon
4 garlic cloves, peeled and thinly sliced
1 bunch fresh thyme, in sprigs
coarse sea salt and freshly ground black pepper
olive oil

Preheat the oven to 425° F.

Prepare the artichokes by first trimming the stems, leaving about 2 in. Peel each stalk down to the paler core. Next break off the tough outer leaves until only the pale tender leaves remain. Trim about 1/2 in off the top. Open the leaves and with a spoon gouge out the choke. If the artichokes are very tender this is not necessary. Rub the lemon over each artichoke to prevent discoloring.

Put a couple of slivers of garlic, a sprig of thyme, and generous salt and pepper into the small cavity in each artichoke. Lay each artichoke on a piece of foil large enough to wrap tightly all around. Drizzle oil over each and season with more salt and pepper. Wrap up tightly in the foil. Roast in the preheated oven for about 30 minutes, or until tender.

Bietola gratinata
Swiss chard gratin

For 6 We adapted this recipe from one published by Lesley Forbes.

3 pounds Swiss chard, leaves and their stalks separated

coarse sea salt and freshly ground black pepper

1/4 cup herb vinegar (Volpaia "Erbe")

3 bay leaves

1 bunch fresh thyme, leaves picked from 1/2 the stalks

4 tablespoons unsalted butter

1 red onion, peeled and sliced

2 garlic cloves, peeled and finely sliced

1 dried red chile, crumbled

20 salted anchovy fillets, prepared (see page 346), 8 fillets kept whole, the rest
    chopped

2 tablespoons all-purpose flour

1/2 nutmeg, freshly grated

1 cup black olives, pitted

1/2 cup freshly grated Parmesan

Preheat the oven to 375° F.

Blanch the chard leaves for 3 minutes in boiling salted water. Drain, keeping the cooking liquid. Slice the chard stalks 1/2 in thick. Put the stalks with 2 1/4 cups of the blanching water in a separate saucepan. Add the vinegar, bay leaves, thyme branches (not the leaves), and black pepper; test for salt. Simmer for 8 minutes. Drain, keeping the cooking liquid.

Melt two tablespoons of the butter in a heavy-bottomed saucepan and fry the onion until soft and beginning to go brown. Add the garlic, chard stalks, thyme leaves, and chile. Fry just to cook the garlic, then add the chopped anchovies. Combine the anchovies with the vegetables, then add the flour, stir, and cook over a low heat for 6-8 minutes. Slowly add the chard cooking liquid, stirring to combine and thicken until you have a thick sauce, the consistency of cream. (You may not need all the liquid.) Season with nutmeg, pepper, and salt if necessary.

Grease an ovenproof or terra-cotta baking dish with a little of the remaining butter. Spread half of the anchovy sauce and chard stalks over the bottom, then carefully cover with the chard leaves. Place over half the olives. Drizzle over the remainder of the anchovy and stalk mixture. Put little bits of butter on top along with the remaining anchovies, the remainder of the olives, and a few thyme leaves. Scatter over the Parmesan.

Bake in the preheated oven for 25 minutes. The top should be colored, the olives slightly roasted.

Patate con finocchio e porcini
Potatoes with fennel and porcini

For 6

6 ounces dried porcini
1/4 cup olive oil
4 garlic cloves, peeled and cut into slivers
8 medium fennel bulbs, trimmed and cut lengthways into 1/2-in slices
3 pounds Yukon Gold potatoes , peeled and cut into 1/2-in slices
coarse sea salt and freshly ground black pepper

Preheat the oven to 400° F.

In this recipe, it is essential that the potatoes, fennel, and porcini are of the same thickness. As they are baked in one layer, a large shallow baking dish should be used.

Soak the porcini in about 2/3 cup hot water for half an hour, then drain carefully through a fine sieve, retaining the soaking water. Heat 1 tablespoon of the oil in a pan, then gently fry the porcini with a little of the garlic for a few minutes. The porcini slices should be slightly browned. Add about 3 tablespoons of the soaking liquid, and continue to cook until soft, and most of the liquid has evaporated.

In a very large saucepan heat the rest of the olive oil, then add the rest of the garlic slivers plus the fennel slices. Cook, stirring, for 5-10 minutes, or until the fennel is soft. Add the potatoes and stir thoroughly, then add the porcini and salt and pepper to taste. Stir together well, then put in one layer in the baking dish. Place in the preheated oven and cook for 30 minutes or until the potatoes are cooked.

Topinambur con parmigiano
Jerusalem artichokes and parmesan

For 6

4 pounds Jerusalem artichokes

1/2 lemon

4 garlic cloves, peeled

3 tablespoons fresh thyme leaves

coarse sea salt

freshly ground black pepper

3 tablespoons unsalted butter

1/2 cup freshly grated Parmesan

2/3 cup Chicken Stock (see page 142)

2/3 cup cream

Preheat the oven to 400° F.

Peel the artichokes and slice lengthways into thick slices. Put the slices in cold water with the half lemon to prevent browning. Remove and dry.

Crush the garlic with the thyme to a fine paste. Mix the artichokes with the paste and season.

Butter a suitable baking dish, and place the artichokes in a couple of layers. Scatter with half the Parmesan. Pour over the stock and dot with the remaining butter. Cover with foil and bake for 20 minutes. Remove the foil, and turn the artichoke slices over. Scatter with the remaining Parmesan, add the cream, and bake for a further 10 minutes. Most of the liquid should have reduced, and the top will be crisp and brown.

Patate e acciughe al forno
Potato and anchovy gratin

For 6

2 pounds Yukon Gold potatoes

2 tablespoons olive oil

2 tablespoons unsalted butter

6 garlic cloves, peeled and sliced

20 salted anchovy fillets, prepared (see page 346)

1 teaspoon finely chopped fresh rosemary

2 dried red chiles, crumbled

1/2 cup freshly grated Parmesan

1 cup cream

coarse sea salt and freshly ground black pepper

3 tablespoons chopped flat-leaf parsley

Preheat the oven to 375° F. Peel the potatoes and cut lengthways into 1/4-in-thick slices. Put into cold water to soak off the starch for 5 minutes.

Heat the oil and butter in a small saucepan. Add the garlic and gently fry for 2 minutes then add the anchovy fillets. Break up and melt the anchovies into a sauce. Add the rosemary and chile. Stir to combine, then remove the pan from the heat.

Drain the potatoes, spread out on a towel, and pat dry. Place in a large bowl and add the anchovy sauce, three-quarters of the Parmesan, and the cream. Season and toss together. Put in a baking dish, cover with foil, and bake in the preheated oven for 25 minutes. Remove the foil, gently turn the potatoes over, then add the parsley. Test for seasoning, then scatter over the remaining Parmesan. Continue to bake for a further 15 minutes. The potatoes should be lightly browned and crisp.

Veget

in pac

ables
lella
7

Carciofi in padella   Frittedda   Piselli, fave, e lenticchi
semi di finocchio   Cicoria brasate   Porri e carciofi bras

sott'olio   Cime di rapa brasate   Cavolo nero brasate con
e   Peperoni in padella   Zucchini, prosciutto, e menta

Carciofi in padella
Artichokes braised with white wine

For 6

12 small young artichokes, with stems attached, prepared (see page 172)
1 lemon, halved
olive oil
1 bunch fresh thyme, leaves picked from the stalks
4 garlic cloves, peeled and thinly sliced
coarse sea salt and freshly ground black pepper
2/3 cup dry white wine

Prepare the artichokes, then rub with a lemon half to prevent discoloring.

In a large heavy saucepan heat 3 tablespoons of the olive oil over a medium heat. Fry the artichokes until they begin to color, then add the thyme and garlic. Season generously with salt and pepper. Stir occasionally.

When the garlic begins to color, add the white wine, the juice from the remaining lemon half, and enough olive oil, about 1/2 cup, to cover. Put the lid on, and simmer gently for about 30 minutes, or until the artichokes are tender.

Frittedda
Braised fava beans, peas, and artichokes

For 6

6 small young artichokes, prepared (see page 172), cut into quarters

2 cups fresh peas, shelled weight (use only young fresh peas)

1 cup fava beans, shelled weight (use only young fresh beans)

2 red onions, peeled and finely sliced

5 tablespoons extra virgin olive oil

2 tablespoons roughly chopped fresh flat-leaf parsley

3 tablespoons roughly chopped fresh mint leaves

coarse sea salt and freshly ground black pepper

juice of 2 lemons

In a large heavy saucepan, gently fry the onion in 2 tablespoons of the oil until golden. Add the artichoke quarters and over a medium heat stir and cook until al dente, about 15 minutes. Add the peas and fava beans and enough water to moisten, about 2/3 cup. Cook until the peas and beans are tender, a further 5-10 minutes.

Stir in the parsley and mint, and season with salt, pepper, lemon juice, and the remainder of the extra virgin olive oil.

Serve at room temperature.

Piselli, fave, e lenticchie sott'olio

For 6

3 pounds each of peas and fava beans in their shells

1 cup Puy or Castelluccio lentils, washed

2 garlic cloves, peeled

extra virgin olive oil

1 lemon, halved

coarse sea salt and freshly ground black pepper

1 large bunch fresh mint, chopped

Shell the peas and fava beans separately, keeping aside any that are particularly large as they take longer to cook.

Cover the lentils with cold water, add the garlic, and bring to the boil. Simmer gently for about 20 minutes until al dente or nutty in texture. Drain, discard the garlic, and toss the lentils in enough olive oil to coat them well, plus a squeeze of lemon juice. Season with salt and pepper.

Blanch the peas first (large, then small) in plenty of salted water for about 1 minute or according to size (the salt keeps the peas green). Drain well, toss while hot with extra virgin olive oil, and season.

Blanch the fava beans in boiling water (*no* salt), and cook for about 2-3 minutes, or longer for the larger ones. Drain well, toss while hot with oil, and season.

Mix the lentils, peas, and fava beans together in a bowl, adding more olive oil if necessary. Add the mint and season once again. Serve warm or at room temperature.

Cime di rapa brasate
Braised broccoli rabe

For 6

4 pounds broccoli rabe
coarse sea salt and freshly ground black pepper
extra virgin olive oil
4 garlic cloves, peeled and finely sliced
2 small dried red chiles, crumbled

Pick through the broccoli rabe and discard any really large, tough outer leaves. Cut off and discard the tough stalks. Keep the sprouting heads and tender leaves. Wash the heads and leaves carefully. Blanch for 5 minutes in boiling salted water. Drain and lay out to dry.

In a heavy-bottomed pan heat 1/4 cup of olive oil, add the garlic slices and dried chile. As the garlic is about to turn in color, add the blanched broccoli rabe and toss for a minute. Season with salt and pepper and serve drizzled with extra virgin olive oil.

188

Cavolo nero brasate con semi di finocchio
Braised cavolo nero with fennel seeds

For 6

4 pounds cavolo nero (or equivalent amount of kale)
coarse sea salt and freshly ground black pepper
extra virgin olive oil
4 garlic cloves, peeled and thinly sliced
20 fennel seeds, crushed

To prepare the cavolo nero, hold the stalk firmly in one hand and strip away the leaves from the stems with the other. Briefly blanch the cavolo leaves in plenty of boiling salted water until they are marginally undercooked, about 5 minutes. They should be a brilliant green color. Drain well and lay out to dry.

Heat enough oil to cover the base of a large saucepan. Add the garlic and gently fry. When it begins to color, add the crushed fennel seeds and fry for a minute more before adding the cavolo nero. Stir-fry for 5 minutes to allow the cavolo to absorb the flavors. Season well and serve.

Cicoria brasate
Braised bitter cicoria

For 6 In Italian markets you can also find puntarelle, part of the same family as cicoria. It is sold when it is sprouting like broccoli and can be cooked in a similar way or eaten as a salad served with warm anchovy sauce (see page 308).

4 pounds cicoria or escarole leaves
coarse sea salt and freshly ground black pepper
3 tablespoons extra virgin olive oil
3 garlic cloves, peeled and thinly sliced
2 small dried red chiles (optional)

To prepare the cicoria, remove the tough outer leaves and then cut the cicoria hearts off at the root. Heat a large pot of boiling salted water, and blanch the cicoria until tender, about 5 minutes. Drain well and lay out to dry.

In a separate pan heat the olive oil and fry the garlic and chile (if using) lightly. Add the cicoria, salt, and pepper, and cook for about 5-10 minutes, stirring.

You can serve this cold, as part of an antipasto, or mixed with some cooked borlotti beans.

Porri e carciofi brasate
Braised leeks and artichokes

For 6

3 pounds leeks
6 small or 3 large artichokes
1 lemon, halved
2 tablespoons olive oil
3 garlic cloves, peeled and finely sliced
2 tablespoons chopped fresh mint leaves
coarse sea salt and freshly ground black pepper
1/2 cup white wine
2-3 tablespoons roughly chopped fresh flat-leaf parsley

Peel the outer leaves from the leeks, and trim the roots and the larger tough green parts. Wash thoroughly and shake dry. Cut the leeks in diagonal dice about 1/2 in thick. Prepare the artichokes as on page 172, until you are left with the pale tender heart. Peel the fiber from the stalks of smaller artichokes; discard the stalks of larger artichokes, as they are too tough. Cut each artichoke heart in eighths and scrape away any choke or prickly violet leaves. Place in a bowl of water with the lemon halves as you cut, then drain and dry.

Heat the oil in a large heavy saucepan with a lid. When hot add the artichoke slices and cook quickly until lightly colored, then add the leeks. Stir-fry together for 5 minutes then add the garlic, mint, salt, and pepper. When the garlic has softened, add the wine and stir to scrape up any artichoke and leek stuck on the bottom. Cover with a lid and cook until the wine has evaporated, about 10-15 minutes. Add the parsley, taste for seasoning, and serve.

Peperoni in padella
Peppers in olive oil

For 6

8 large ripe dark red peppers
1/4 cup olive oil
coarse sea salt and freshly ground black pepper
3 tablespoons herb wine vinegar (Volpaia "Erbe")

Wash and dry the peppers, then cut in half lengthways and then in half again and again. Using a small paring knife, remove any white membrane on the inside of the peppers, plus the seeds.

Use a large frying pan or low-sided large saucepan with a lid. Heat half the olive oil and place some of the pepper pieces in one layer. Fry over a medium to high heat with the lid on, turning the pieces over as they begin to color and become soft. Remove with a slotted spoon and keep warm. Repeat with a second layer of peppers, and continue until you have cooked them all. You may have to use extra oil if you fry in more than two batches. Drain off excess oil.

Return all the peppers to the pan, reheat together, and season with salt, pepper, and vinegar.

Zucchini, Prosciutto, e Menta

For 6

2 pounds zucchini
3 garlic cloves, peeled
3-4 tablespoons olive oil
coarse sea salt and freshly ground black pepper
1 large bunch mint, leaves removed from the stalks, coarsely chopped
9 slices prosciutto, cut into wide strips
extra virgin olive oil

Trim the ends of the zucchini, cut lengthways into quarters and then again into 1 1/2-in pieces, slicing diagonally with your knife. If the garlic cloves are small, leave whole; if not, cut in half lengthways.

In a heavy-bottomed frying pan with a lid, heat the olive oil over a moderate flame. Add the garlic, the zucchini, salt, and pepper, and toss. Cook the zucchini until tender but crisp and slightly brown, about 15 minutes.

Remove from the heat, place all the mint leaves evenly over the zucchini, followed by the prosciutto. Immediately cover with the tight-fitting lid, and let sit until ready to serve.

Drizzle with extra virgin olive oil, season again, and toss gently. Serve at room temperature.

Fish
Shel

lfish

8

Zuppa di pesce
Fish soup

For 8

3 small lobsters, each about 1 pound in weight, halved

5-ounce fillets of red snapper or red mullet, scaled

1 pound mussels or clams, scrubbed

12 prawns or langoustines

1/4 cup olive oil

2 small red onions, peeled and finely chopped

3 garlic cloves, peeled and chopped

1-2 tablespoons dried oregano

3 small dried red chiles, crumbled

3 pounds ripe plum or other tomatoes, peeled, seeded, and roughly chopped

1 cup white wine

12 medium Yukon Gold or other yellow potatoes, scrubbed and cut into 2-in pieces

coarse sea salt and freshly ground black pepper

1/4 cup chopped fresh flat-leaf parsley

8 crostini (see page 290)

extra virgin olive oil

Heat the olive oil in a very large heavy saucepan big enough to hold all the fish, or two medium to large pans.

Add the onion and fry gently until soft and turning gold, then add the garlic, oregano, and chile, and cook for 2 minutes. Add the tomato and continue to cook gently.

When the tomato begins to break up, add the wine, bring to the boil, then add the potato. Cook the potato for 5 minutes, then add the lobsters. Put the lid on and simmer gently for 3-4 minutes, then add the snapper or mullet fillets and carry on simmering for a further 5 minutes.

Add the mussels or clams and the prawns. Season with salt and pepper, replace the lid, and simmer for a further 5-6 minutes. The mussels or clams should have opened (discard any that remain closed), and the fish should be perfectly cooked. Add the chopped parsley to the liquor.

Serve with crostini drizzled with extra virgin olive oil.

Gamberetti fritti
Deep-fried shrimps

For 6 Poole prawns are in season from June to September in a warm summer, and are caught in pots that the Dorset fishermen make specially for the purpose. The prawns are brown, about 1 1/2 in long excluding the whiskers, and are sold live.

3 1/4 pounds live Poole prawns or similar shrimps about 1 inch long
sunflower oil for deep-frying
coarse sea salt and freshly ground black pepper

Chile sauce
4 medium to large fresh red chiles, seeded and finely chopped
3/4 cup extra virgin olive oil
juice of 1 lemon

Herb salad
10 ounces mixed herb leaves (dill, red and green basil, mint, arugula)
1/4 cup of extra virgin olive oil
3 tablespoons of lemon juice

For the chile sauce, mix the ingredients together and season with salt and pepper.

To prepare the prawns – which are eaten whole – cut off the unicorn spike on the head of each, using scissors.

Heat the oil to 350° F. Deep-fry the prawns in batches that will fit into your fryer, just for 1 minute. They will turn bright pink as they cook. Drain well on paper towels, then season generously with salt and pepper.

Serve the prawns hot with the chile sauce and dressed herb salad.

Cozze al forno con zucchini, capperi, e peperoni

Baked mussels with zucchini, capers, and peppers

For 6

6 pounds mussels, thoroughly cleaned

1/4 cup olive oil

1 medium red onion, peeled and finely sliced

4 garlic cloves, peeled and finely sliced

2 small dried red chiles, crumbled

2/3 cup dry white wine

2 pounds ripe plum tomatoes, skinned, seeded and chopped, or 1 28-ounce can
    peeled plum tomatoes, drained of their juices

coarse sea salt and freshly ground black pepper

3 small zucchini, trimmed

3 yellow peppers

1/4 cup salted capers, prepared (see page 346), and then soaked in 3 tablespoons
    red wine vinegar

6 tablespoons chopped fresh flat-leaf parsley

extra virgin olive oil

2 lemons

Preheat the oven to 450° F.

In a large saucepan heat the olive oil and gently fry the onion until soft and beginning to color. Add the garlic, cook for a minute, then add the dried red chile, half the white wine, and the tomatoes. Cook together for half an hour – the sauce should have begun to thicken. Season generously.

Cut the zucchini in half lengthways and then into 1/8-in slices. In a separate pan of boiling salted water, blanch the zucchini for just 1 minute. Drain immediately.

Grill the peppers on all sides until the skin is black, then cool in a plastic bag. When cool, remove the skins, seeds, and any thick white fibers from the insides. Cut the flesh into 1/2 in cubes.

Use a large open casserole, high-sided roasting pan, or an ovenproof saucepan. Spoon the tomato sauce on to the bottom of the pan. Add the capers, cover with the mussels, the zucchini, and peppers. Pour over the remaining white wine, shake over half the parsley, and drizzle with a little extra virgin olive oil. Place in the hot oven and bake for 10 minutes or until all the mussels have opened, discarding any that remain closed.

Serve in large flat soup bowls with the remainder of the parsley, more extra virgin olive oil, and a slice of lemon.

Aragosta al forno
Wood-roasted lobster

For 6

6 live lobsters, weighing about 1 1/4 pounds each
coarse sea salt and freshly ground black pepper
2 dried red chiles, crumbled
1 tablespoon dried oregano
3 lemons
1/4 cup extra virgin olive oil
3 large red fresh chiles, seeded and chopped
1/4 cup chopped flat-leaf parsley
6 lemon wedges

Preheat the oven to 475° F.

Place the live lobsters face down on a board. Use a large sharp pointed knife to split them down the center. Remove the little sac found near the head. Crack the claws so that you can easily pick the flesh out when the lobster is cooked.

Season the flesh of the lobsters with salt, pepper, and dried chile, sprinkle with oregano, and squeeze over the juice of 2 lemons. Place on baking sheets and roast in the preheated very hot oven for 15 minutes. The shell of the lobster should turn red and the flesh should gently brown.

Mix the oil with the chopped fresh chile and parsley, then add a tablespoon of lemon juice. Drizzle this sauce over each lobster. Serve with lemon wedges.

Insalata di polpa di granchio
Crab salad

For 6 Live crabs should be kept in the fridge so they are cold and go to sleep.

3 live crabs, about 2-3 pounds each in weight
coarse sea salt and freshly ground black pepper
juice of 2 lemons
6 tablespoons extra virgin olive oil
4 medium fresh chiles, seeded and chopped
1 small bunch green fennel herb, roughly chopped
6 lemon wedges
a handful of arugula
6 sourdough bruschetta (see page 290)

Put each crab in its own large saucepan of cold water. Add 2 ounces of salt to each pan, cover, and very slowly bring the water to the boil. The crabs are cooked when the water reaches boiling point. Remove the crabs from the pans, drain, and leave to cool.

Break each crab open by pulling away the upper body shell. Scrape out the meat and put into a bowl. Break the claws and legs from the body, crack, and pick out the meat, keeping the pieces as large as possible.

Mix two-thirds of the lemon juice with the oil and chile, then season. Add the crabmeat. Season with salt, pepper, and the remaining lemon juice only.

Cover half of each bruschetta generously with dark crabmeat and half with white meat. Sprinkle over the fennel, and serve with a lemon wedge and arugula.

Baccalà
Salt cod

For 6 It is best to buy a whole cod – of about 5-6 pounds, say – and to take it home and fillet it yourself. It is important that the salting process is started the moment you have finished filleting in order to prevent deterioration of the cut side of the fish.

2 pounds very fresh fillet of cod with skin intact
2 pounds natural coarse sea salt

Use a flat board, and arrange this in a tray, with a saucer placed under one end to make it slant at an angle.

Cover the board with a layer of salt about 1/2 in deep. Place the fish, skin side down, on top of the salt. Cover the other side of the fish with 1/2 in of salt. Put in the fridge for 24 hours minimum – 5 days maximum.

Remove the salt by rinsing the fish under a running cold tap for 5 minutes. Then place in a bath of water for 6 hours, changing the water as frequently as possible.

Inzimino di baccalà
Salt cod with chickpeas

For 6

1 1/2 pounds salt cod (see page 212), cut into 2-in pieces

1 cup dried chickpeas, soaked overnight

1 large potato, peeled

5 large garlic cloves, peeled, and 3 sliced finely

1 sprig each of fresh thyme, bay, and sage

3 tablespoons olive oil

2 small dried red chiles, crumbled

1 28-ounce can peeled plum tomatoes, drained of their juices

coarse sea salt and freshly ground black pepper

2 pounds Swiss chard, large stems removed, blanched and roughly chopped

1 cup white wine

3 tablespoons chopped fresh flat-leaf parsley

Put the chickpeas into a saucepan with the potato, 2 whole garlic cloves, and the herbs. Cover with cold water, bring to the boil, and skim the surface. Turn the heat down and simmer for 1-1 1/2 hours. Keep the chickpeas in their cooking liquid until you use them.

Heat 2 tablespoons of oil in a heavy-bottomed pan. Add half the sliced garlic, cook to soften a little, then add half the chile and the tomatoes. Cook for 30 minutes. Season.

Heat the remaining oil in a heavy-bottomed pan. Add the rest of the garlic and fry briefly. Place the cod on the garlic, brown on both sides, then add the wine. Reduce the heat and simmer for a few minutes until the cod is cooked. Season with pepper and chile. Add the skinned chickpeas (see page 346) to the tomato sauce. Gently heat for 2-3 minutes then add the chard and the cod, with the pan juices. Sprinkle with the parsley.

Insalata di baccalà
Salt cod salad

For 6

3 pounds baccalà (salt cod, see page 212)

1 small bunch parsley, leaves picked from the stalks, roughly chopped (keep the
   stalks for the stock)

coarse sea salt and freshly ground black pepper

1 garlic clove, peeled and crushed with a little salt

juice of 3 lemons

1/2 cup extra virgin olive oil

6 fresh red chiles, seeded and chopped

1 bunch arugula, washed and dried

1 cup black Niçoise olives, pitted

6 bruschetta (see page 290)

Stock

4 fresh bay leaves

1 fennel bulb, cut into 4, including the green parts, or a handful of fresh fennel leaves

1/2 whole head garlic

2 carrots, peeled

1 small red onion, peeled

1/2 head celery

2 tablespoons black peppercorns

Soak the salt cod in fresh water, changing the water as many times as possible, for at least 48 hours. Drain thoroughly.

Put the cod in a large pot with the stock ingredients and the stalks of the parsley. Cover with cold water, bring to the boil, and very gently simmer until the cod is tender and flakes easily, about 15-20 minutes. Drain well and leave to cool.

When cool enough to handle, pull the cod apart into flakes. Put in a bowl and season with black pepper to taste, the salt-crushed garlic, and a little of the lemon juice and olive oil. Turn the cod over once or twice in the bowl to season each flake, then add the chopped parsley leaves and the chile.

Put the arugula in a large serving bowl and toss with the remaining olive oil and lemon juice, then add the seasoned salt cod. Scatter over the olives. Turn gently together to combine, and serve with bruschetta.

Strati di sardine
Layered sardine sandwich

For 6 The following quantity of sardines will give you six fillets per portion; you might want to do eight fillets per person for a main course.

18 large very fresh sardines

olive oil

1/2 cup bread crumbs

grated zest of 2 lemons

1 cup pine nuts

3 small dried red chiles, crumbled

1 bunch fresh flat-leaf parsley, leaves picked from their stalks, finely chopped

coarse sea salt and freshly ground black pepper

3 lemons, thickly sliced

Preheat the oven to 400° F.

First scale the sardines, then slit the stomach with your knife and remove the guts. Cut the head off, following the angle of the gills. Make an incision with your knife, cutting in toward the backbone, and along the spine of the fish, carefully cutting the fillet away from the bone. Repeat on the other side. Sardines have a lot of very fine bones which are attached to the backbone. Trim any large bones that remain on the fillets.

Brush a baking sheet with olive oil and lay three of the fillets skin side down next to each other. Sprinkle with some of the bread crumbs, lemon zest, pine nuts, dried chile, parsley, salt, and pepper. Then lay another three fillets directly over the top, skin side up. Sprinkle with more bread crumbs, lemon zest, dried chile, parsley, pine nuts, salt, and pepper. This is one portion. Repeat this process until you have six sandwiches.

Drizzle the sandwiches lightly with olive oil and bake in the preheated oven for about 6-8 minutes. Serve with lemon slices.

Trigliette al vino bianco, prezzemolo, e aglio
Red snapper with white wine, parsley, and garlic

For 6

12 small red snapper, scaled and cleaned
6 tablespoons olive oil
1 small bunch fresh flat-leaf parsley, finely chopped
3 garlic cloves, peeled and finely chopped
3/4 bottle white wine
6 pugliese bruschetta (see page 290)

Preheat the oven to 450° F.

In a small frying pan heat the olive oil, and cook the parsley and the garlic over low heat until soft.

Arrange the snapper in a roasting pan, then pour in the wine along with the oil, parsley, and garlic. Place over moderate heat and bring just to the boil, then put in the preheated oven for 10 minutes.

Put a piece of bruschetta and 2 red snappers on each plate, and serve immediately.

Calamari ripiene con peperoncino al forno
Wood-roasted squid stuffed with chile

For 6 as a starter

6 squid, the size of an adult hand, about 8 in
juice of 2 lemons and 3 whole lemons, halved
1/2 cup extra virgin olive oil
5 large fresh red chiles, seeded and chopped
coarse sea salt and freshly ground black pepper
1 garlic clove, peeled and finely chopped
3 tablespoons chopped fresh flat-leaf parsley
1 tablespoon dried oregano
1 bunch arugula, washed and dried

Preheat the oven to 450° F.

Clean the squid by pulling the tentacles and head away from the body. Turn the body sac inside out and scrape away the guts remaining. Turn the body sac right side out again. Cut the head and beak off the tentacles, and discard.

Mix 2 tablespoons of the lemon juice with 4 tablespoons of the olive oil, then add half the chile, some salt and pepper, and the garlic. Stir in 1 tablespoon of the chopped parsley. Put some of this mixture inside each squid, dividing it equally. Mix the rest of the chile with 3 tablespoons of the remaining olive oil, and season.

Heat a large baking dish, and brush with the rest of the olive oil. Sprinkle the oregano and some salt and pepper over each squid, then place in the hot oil. Turn over and place in the oven. Roast for 5-6 minutes; they should be slightly brown. Serve with the chile sauce, the remaining parsley, arugula, and lemon halves.

Spiedini di coda di rospo e cappesante
Spiedini of monkfish and scallops

For 6

12 medium fresh scallops
2 pounds monkfish, boned and skinned
6-in rosemary branches
coarse sea salt and freshly ground black pepper
Anchovy and Rosemary Sauce (see page 308)
2 lemons, cut into wedges

For each spiedino you need 2 scallops and 2 cubes of monkfish. Pull the leaves off the rosemary stalks, leaving just the tufts at the end. Sharpen the other end into a point.

To prepare the scallops, place them, flat shell side down, on a board. Insert a sharp knife close to the hinge and pry open. Remove the whole scallop from the bottom shell by gently cutting, keeping the blade flat; use a gentle sawing motion. The whole scallop will now be cupped in the top curved half of the shell. Use a tablespoon and carefully scoop out the scallop; trim off the membrane. Wash, then pat dry.

Cut the monkfish into cubes roughly the same size as the scallops. Thread a scallop on first, making sure the rosemary stick goes through the white muscle part and the coral. Next thread on a piece of monkfish, then the other scallop, and finally the other piece of monkfish.

Heat a grill. When very hot, place the spiedini on and grill. Season with salt and pepper while grilling. Turn over after 3 minutes or when the spiedini no longer stick but have sealed and are brown. Grill for a further few minutes.

Serve the spiedini with Anchovy and Rosemary Sauce, along with wedges of lemon.

Salmone selvatico fiammeggiato
Seared wild salmon

For 6

1 8-pound wild salmon
coarse sea salt and freshly ground black pepper
3 lemons

Place the salmon on its side on a board. With a very sharp filleting knife, slice the head off behind the gills. You will expose the main bone. Place one hand on the top side of the salmon to keep it in place and with your other hand cut along the top of the bone, keeping the blade of your knife angled toward the bone, using the finger and thumb of your other hand to lift the side of salmon away as you cut. You will be cutting through the small fillet bones as you go. Turn the salmon over and repeat the process. Remove the pinbones with tweezers. Trim the belly sides of the fillets free of fat.

To portion your pieces of salmon, place one side skin-side down on your board. You are aiming to get six portions altogether, three from each fillet. Divide the side equally into three by eye, and cut into the salmon at about a 45-degree angle, cutting straight through the skin at the bottom.

Season your pieces of salmon with salt and pepper, and grill skin-side down first on a preheated very hot grill pan or grill for about 1 minute until just seared. Turn over and sear the flesh side. Serve with wedges of lemon.

Salmone selvatico al sale
Wild salmon baked whole in sea salt

For 8

1 8-pound whole wild salmon, scaled and cleaned
Maldon salt and freshly ground black pepper
1 large bunch fresh fennel leaves and stalks, washed
10-12 pounds coarse sea salt

Preheat the oven to 425° F.

Season the salmon well with pepper and salt on the inside only. Fill the gut cavity with the fresh fennel leaves and stalks (there is no need to chop them up).

Cover the bottom of a large roasting pan with a layer of salt 1/2 in deep. Place the salmon on the salt. Pile the salt over the fish so that it is completely covered by at least 1/2 in all over. Do not worry if the head and tail protrude.

Sprinkle a few tablespoons of water over the surface of the salt.

Place the salmon in the hot oven and bake for about 20 minutes. To test if the fish is cooked, pierce the salt with a skewer and into the fish at a place where the fish is thickest. If it is warm, the salmon is cooked. Remove from the oven, and allow to cool to a temperature you can handle.

Break off the salt crust from the top of the fish; the skin should have stuck to the salt and come away as you do this. Gently lift the whole fish out of the roasting pan. Peel away any skin and salt stuck to the underside and place the fish on a board.

Pull the fillets off the bones. Serve at room temperature with Basil Mayonnaise or Anchovy-Caper Mayonnaise, or Salsa Verde (see pages 310 and 311).

Rombo con rosmarino al sale
Whole turbot with rosemary baked in sea salt

For 6 Buy a fresh turbot that is not thick with roe and still has sea slime on its skin. Have the fishmonger remove only the gut.

1 turbot with head and tail intact, about 6-7 pounds
7 1/2 pounds natural coarse sea salt
1 bunch fresh rosemary
freshly ground black pepper
balsamic vinegar (aged and thick)
extra virgin olive oil
3 lemons

Preheat the oven to 425° F.

Use a large baking pan that will snugly hold the turbot. Cover the bottom with a layer of salt, and place the turbot on the salt. Push the rosemary into the cavity and completely cover the fish with the remainder of the salt, about 3/4 in thick. Do not worry if the head and tail protrude. Sprinkle the surface of the salt very lightly with a little water – use a few tablespoons.

Place in the preheated oven and bake for 25-35 minutes. After 20 minutes test by inserting a skewer into the center of the fish; if it is warm, the turbot is cooked.

Allow to cool for 5 minutes, then crack open the salt crust. Carefully remove as much of the salt as possible. You will find the thick skin of the turbot will stick to the salt.

Serve at room temperature, with coarsely ground black pepper, a few dribbles of balsamic vinegar, extra virgin olive oil, and a half lemon.

Trancio di rombo al forno con capperi
Wood-roasted turbot tranche with capers

For 6

6 slices turbot or monkfish on the bone, about 8-10 ounces each
2 tablespoons olive oil
coarse sea salt and freshly ground black pepper
juice of 3 lemons
6 tablespoons chopped green celery leaves (the younger leaves are best)
6 tablespoons chopped fresh flat-leaf parsley
1/2 cup salted capers, prepared (see page 346)
1 lemon, sliced

Preheat the oven to 450° F.

Brush the fish lightly with olive oil, and season with salt and pepper. Place in one layer on a shallow baking pan. Bake in the preheated oven for 15-20 minutes, according to the size of the slices.

Remove from the oven and put the fish on serving plates. Add the lemon juice, celery leaves, half the parsley, and the capers to the baking pan, and heat for about a minute over a high flame to combine the fish juices with the lemon juice.

Serve, pouring the capers and the juices over the turbot. Sprinkle the remainder of the parsley on top, and serve with a slice of lemon.

Branzino ripieno d'erbe
Sea bass slashed and stuffed with herbs

For 6

1 sea bass, about 7-8 pounds in weight, scaled and cleaned, or 6 6-7-ounce individual
    sea bass fillets
coarse sea salt and freshly ground black pepper
2 tablespoons each of fresh marjoram, fresh basil or mint, and fresh green fennel or
    dill, roughly chopped
3 lemons
6 tablespoons extra virgin olive oil

Preheat the grill. It must be very hot and clean.

Make 1/2-in deep slashes across the width of the whole sea bass at 2 1/2 in intervals. Slash the skin side of the fillets in the same way. Season the fish with salt and pepper. Mix the herbs together and then push as much of this mixture into the slashes as you can.

Place the whole fish on the grill and do not turn over until it is completely sealed. Turn over when the fish comes away easily. When sealed on both sides, reduce the heat and continue grilling until the fish is cooked. Alternatively, grill the fillets, skin side down first, on the grill.

Mix the juice of 1 of the lemons with the olive oil, and pour over the grilled fish, then scatter any remaining herbs over. Serve with lemon wedges.

Sogliola al forno con origano e alloro
Roasted dover sole with oregano and bay

For 6

6 whole Dover sole, weighing about 12-14 ounces each, scaled and cleaned
extra virgin olive oil
6 lemons
24 dried bay leaves
1/4 cup dried wild oregano
coarse sea salt and coarsely ground black pepper

Preheat the oven to 450° F.

Brush shallow baking pans with olive oil. Slice 2 of the lemons into fine rounds 1/8 in thick. Scatter half the bay leaves, a few of the lemon slices, and some oregano on the bottom of the pans. Place the soles on top, season generously with salt and pepper, then scatter the remaining dried oregano, bay leaves, and lemon slices on top of the fish to cover them. Drizzle generously with olive oil and bake in the preheated oven for 15-20 minutes. Test using the point of a sharp knife down the center of the thickest part of the sole; if cooked, the flesh should just be coming away from the bone.

When cooked, remove the sole from the baking pans, and place on serving plates. Place the baking tray with its remaining herbs and fish juices over a medium heat and deglaze with the juice from 3 of the remaining lemons. Serve each sole with some of this sauce from the pan, the herb leaves, and lemon wedges.

Tonno marinato e fiammeggiato
Seared marinated tuna

For 6

6 pieces fresh bluefin tuna about 3/4 in thick, and about 6 ounces each in weight

3 garlic cloves, peeled and finely chopped

1 bunch fresh green fennel

1 teaspoon fennel seeds, ground in a mortar

2 small dried red chiles, crumbled

coarse sea salt and freshly ground black pepper

3/4 cup white wine

6 tablespoons olive oil

4 lemons

Place the tuna steaks on a board. Rub half the garlic into the fish, along with half the chopped fennel, fennel seeds, chile, and salt and pepper. Turn over and do the same on the other side.

Place the steaks side by side in a large flat container, and pour in the white wine, olive oil, and the juice of 1 lemon. Cover and leave to marinate in a cool place for at least 1 hour.

Preheat the grill, and sear the tuna for only 1 minute on each side.

Serve hot with a wedge of lemon, and a sauce – Fresh Red Chile and Fennel Sauce or Green Chile and Lemon Peel Sauce (see pages 306 and 305).

Lombo di tonno al forno con coriandolo
Baked whole loin of tuna with coriander

For 8

6 pounds tuna loin in one piece, skin removed

4 garlic cloves, peeled and cut into slivers

3 tablespoons coriander seeds, lightly crushed

coarse sea salt and freshly ground black pepper

1 bunch fresh mint, leaves picked from the stalks, roughly chopped

1/4 cup extra virgin olive oil

1/2 bottle white wine

1/4 cup salted capers, prepared (see page 346)

Tomato Sauce

3 pounds ripe plum tomatoes, skinned, seeded, and roughly chopped

3 tablespoons olive oil

4 garlic cloves, peeled and finely chopped

2-3 dried red chiles, crumbled

1 3-in cinnamon stick

1 teaspoon dried oregano

1 bunch fresh mint, leaves picked from the stalks, roughly chopped

2 large fresh red chiles, seeded and chopped

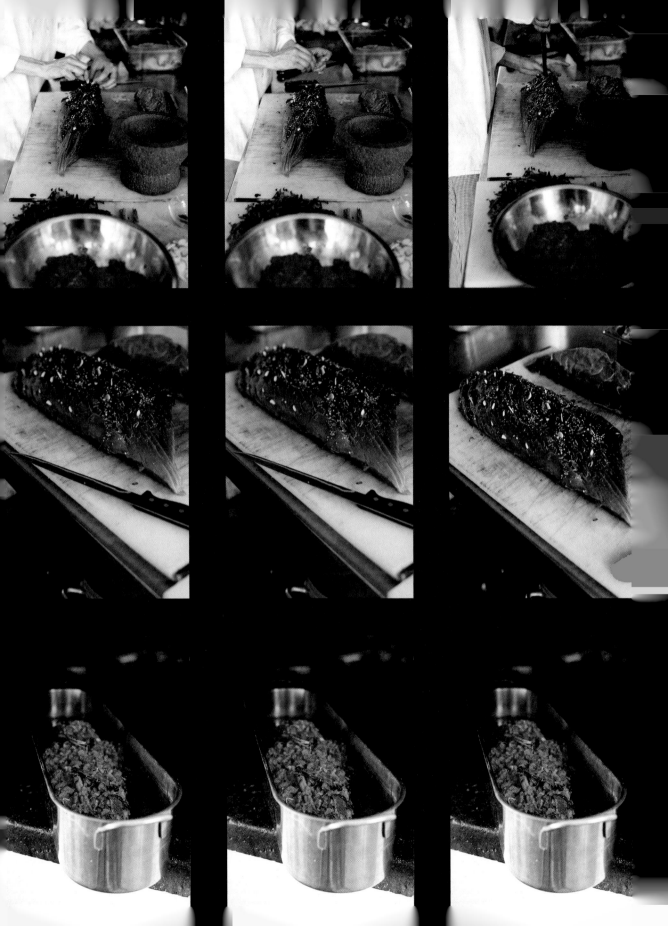

Trim the tuna loin of any sinew and very dark flesh, and skin it. To stud the loin, using a small sharp kitchen knife, make horizontal slits along the complete surface of the tuna, about 2 in apart, and 3/4 in deep. The flesh of a tuna has a natural flakiness; make sure you follow that when making the incisions. Into each slit push a sliver of garlic, a little coriander, some salt and pepper, and finally a little mint. This will take time as you must split and stuff all sides of the loin.

Preheat the oven to 425° F.

To make the tomato sauce, heat the olive oil in a large heavy-bottomed pan. Add the garlic, dried chile, the whole cinnamon stick, oregano, and remaining coriander and fry together until the garlic begins to turn golden in color. Then add the mint followed by the tomatoes and fresh chile. Stir and cook together over the high heat for 10-15 minutes. The flavors should blend and the tomatoes should reduce a little. Season with salt and pepper.

Take a casserole or heavy-bottomed roasting pan, and heat the oil in it until very hot. Place the tuna in the pan and seal and brown on all sides. Remove the loin from the pan and pour off excess oil. Pour the wine into the pan to deglaze it, and allow to reduce a little, stirring and scraping. Return the tuna loin to the pan, and pour over the tomato sauce. This may not completely cover the loin; spoon some of the liquid over the top. Half cover the casserole, and put in the preheated oven to bake for up to 20 minutes or until cooked (rare tuna is delicious).

Place the loin on a large carving board and slice into thick slices. Serve with the tomato sauce, and sprinkled with the remaining chopped mint and the capers.

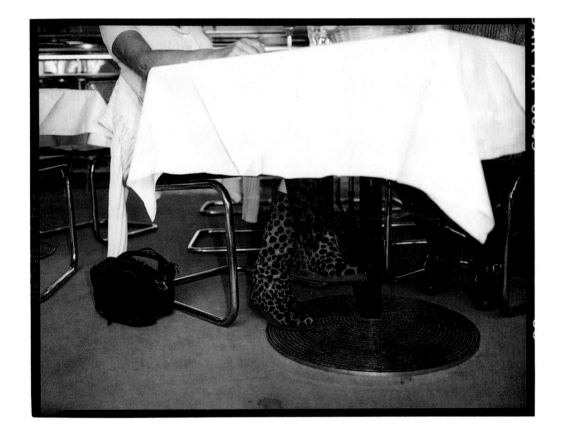

Pork C

Duck G

hicken

Game

9

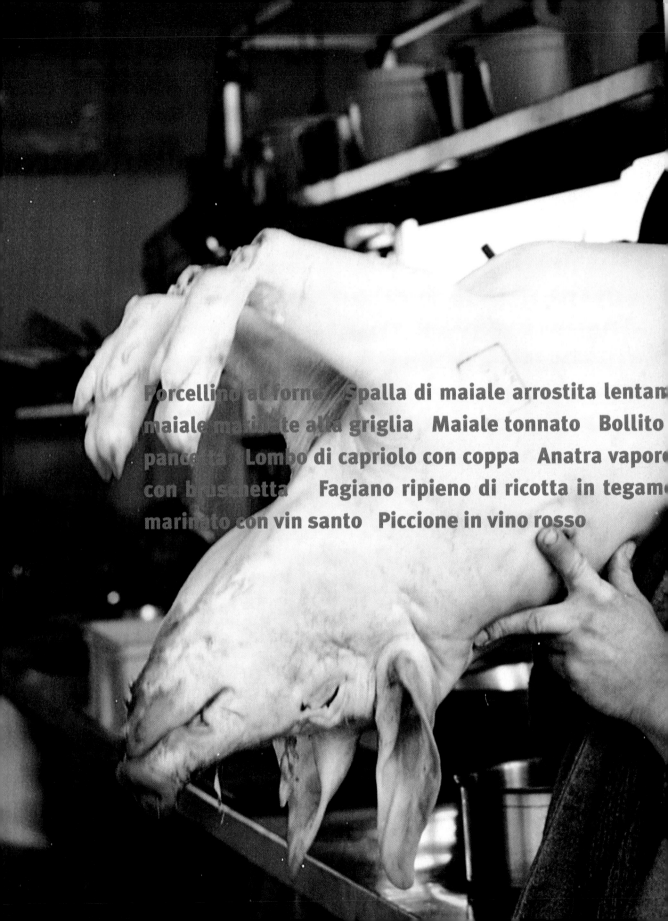

Porcellino al forno Spalla di maiale arrostita lentam
maiale marinate alla griglia Maiale tonnato Bollito
pancetta Lombo di capriolo con coppa Anatra vapor
con bruschetta Fagiano ripieno di ricotta in tegam
marinato con vin santo Piccione in vino rosso

ente   Lonza di maiale arrosto nella cotenna   Costate di
nisto   Faraona costata e maggiorana   Pollo al sale con
e arrosto   Tetraone marinato al ginepro   Tetraone ripiene
Pernice con timo e mascarpone   Piccione alla griglia

Porcellino al forno
Wood-roasted suckling pig

For 8 An eight-week-old pig weighs about 16 pounds. Pigs of 20 pounds plus have more flavor, but they are too big for most domestic ovens. Order a pig that has had a cereal feed supplement for at least two weeks; this adds texture and taste.

1 suckling pig
6 garlic cloves, peeled
1/4 cup fennel seeds
coarse sea salt and coarsely ground black pepper
2 bunches fresh rosemary, leaves picked from the stalks
olive oil
1 1/2 cups Chicken Stock (see page 142) or water
1/2 bottle red wine

Preheat the oven to 450° F.

Crush the garlic in a mortar with the fennel seeds and 3 tablespoons salt. Add the rosemary leaves a little at a time, crushing together to make a rough paste. Add 2 tablespoons pepper.

Make fine scores in the skin of the pig wherever there is fat beneath the skin (very young pigs have practically no fat, so scoring is not possible). Rub the whole pig inside and out with the paste and into the scores. Brush with olive oil.

Place the pig on its side on a rack in a large roasting pan. You may have to curl it round to fit. Place in the hot oven and roast for 15 minutes, just to allow the skin to crackle, then carefully turn the pig on to its other side and roast for a further 15 minutes. The skin should be crisp on both sides.

Add the stock or water to the roasting pan. Turn the oven down to 325° F and, basting from time to time, roast for 2 1/2-3 hours – longer if the pig is 20 pounds and over. The pig is cooked when the shoulders and legs can be easily pulled away from the body.

Place the pig on a large preheated serving tray and set aside.

Remove as much fat as you can from the roasting pan. Place the roasting pan on the direct heat, add the red wine, and stir briskly to incorporate the meat juices. Season.

When carving the pig, place thick slices cut from the leg and shoulder and some rib chops on each plate along with a piece of crackling. Pour over each plate a little of the meat juices. Serve with wood-roasted vegetables (see pages 146-179) and Salsa Verde (see page 311).

Spalla di maiale arrostita lentamente
Slow-roasted shoulder of pork

For 8-10 Shoulder of pork is the most suitable cut of pork for this long method of cooking, as the meat is layered with fat which slowly melts away. We cook it overnight in the cooling wood oven.

1 small whole shoulder of pork, with skin, about 6-7 pounds in weight
10 garlic cloves, peeled
1/2 cup fennel seeds
coarse sea salt and freshly ground black pepper
5-6 small dried red chiles, crumbled
juice of 5 lemons
3 tablespoons olive oil

Preheat the oven to 450° F. Using a small sharp knife, score the whole skin of the shoulder with deep cuts about 1/4 in wide.

Smash the garlic with the fennel seeds, then mix with salt, pepper, and chile to taste. Rub and push this mixture into and over the skin and all the surfaces of the meat. Place the shoulder on a rack in a roasting pan and roast for 30 minutes or until the skin begins to crackle, blister, and brown. Turn the shoulder and pour on half the lemon juice and 2 tablespoons of the oil. Turn the oven down, to 250° F, and leave the meat to roast, overnight or all day (from 8-24 hours). Turn over occasionally and baste with extra lemon juice and, if necessary, a little oil.

The shoulder is ready when it is completely soft under the crisp skin. You can tell by pushing with your finger: the meat will give way and might even fall off the bone. Serve each person with some of the crisp skin and meat cut from different parts of the shoulder. Add extra lemon juice to deglaze the pan, and spoon this over.

Lonza di maiale avvolta nella cotenna
Roast loin of pork wrapped in crackling

For 6-8 This loin of pork is a successful alternative to a whole suckling pig.

1/2 whole loin of pork with skin, rib end, about 6-7 pounds in weight, boned
10 garlic cloves, peeled
1/4 cup fennel seeds
coarse sea salt and coarsely ground black pepper
juice of 2 lemons
2 tablespoons olive oil

Preheat the oven to 450° F.

Using a small sharp knife, score the skin of the loin with deep cuts about 1/4 in apart. Remove the scored skin from the loin, leaving only a thin layer of fat.

Smash the garlic in a pestle and mortar with the fennel seeds, then mix with 3 tablespoons sea salt and 1 tablespoon pepper. Rub and push this mixture into and over the skin and all the surfaces of the loin. Wrap the scored skin over the loin and tie on securely with string.

Place the loin on a rack in a roasting pan and put into the hot oven. Allow the skin to crackle, blister, and brown. Turn the loin and pour on half the lemon juice and 2 tablespoons of the oil. Turn the oven down to 400° F, and roast for 40 minutes. Every now and then turn over and baste with the juices. Turn the oven off and leave the loin in the oven with the door partially open for a further 25 minutes.

Serve each person with some of the crisp skin and meat cut from either end of the loin. Add a little lemon juice to deglaze the pan and spoon this over the meat.

Costate di maiale marinate alla griglia
Grilled marinated pork chops

For 6 Make sure the chops are cut from the center loin which includes the fillet.

6 pork chops, about 1 in thick, fat removed

4 garlic cloves, peeled

3 tablespoons coarse sea salt

2 tablespoons black peppercorns, coarsely ground

6 sprigs rosemary, leaves picked from the stalks, roughly chopped

juice of 3 lemons

6 tablespoons olive oil

6 lemon wedges

Place each chop on a piece of plastic wrap at least 10 in square, and cover with a second piece of plastic wrap. Using a wooden mallet, gently beat the chops to flatten them out until doubled in size. This takes time and patience. The beaten chops should be about 1/2 in thick. Place in a container large enough to hold them in one layer.

In a mortar, roughly pound the garlic with the salt, pepper, and rosemary. Add the lemon juice and olive oil to liquefy the mixture. Spread this marinade over both sides of each chop, and leave in a cool place, covered, for about 1 hour.

Preheat the grill, and grill each chop for 5-6 minutes on each side. Serve with lemon.

Maiale tonnato
Pork tonnato

For 6 You can make this dish with leftover Roast Loin of Pork Wrapped in Crackling (see page 250), or cook the pork as below a day in advance.

about 5-6 pounds rump end of loin of pork on the bone (or as above)

6 garlic cloves, peeled

1 bunch rosemary, leaves picked from the stalks

coarse sea salt and freshly ground black pepper

juice of 1 lemon

1 7-ounce can Italian tuna in olive oil

1 recipe Anchovy-Caper Mayonnaise (see page 311)

12 salted anchovy fillets, prepared (see page 346)

1/2 cup salted capers, prepared (see page 346)

3 tablespoons small basil leaves

Preheat the oven to 450° F.

Trim the fat from the top side of the pork, leaving about 1/2 in only. With a small sharp pointed knife, make small incisions along and around each rib bone. Using a pestle and mortar, crush the garlic, rosemary leaves, and 2 tablespoons salt together to make a crude paste. Rub this paste into all the cuts and over the fat.

Place the loin on a roasting rack in a roasting pan and roast in the preheated hot oven. Turn the pork over after 20 minutes, and baste. Turn the oven down to 400° F, and continue to roast and baste for a further hour.

Remove the rack from the pan. Put the meat in the pan, pour over the lemon juice, baste for a final time, and return to the oven for a further 10-15 minutes. The meat should be cooked just beyond pink. Remove from the oven and allow to cool in the roasting pan – for at least 2 hours.

When the meat is completely cold, carefully cut the loin away from the bones. Try to keep it in one piece. Keep the solidified juices from the pan.

Trim any fat from the loin and carve the meat into very fine slices. Arrange these overlapping on a large serving plate. Spread the solidified meat juices over the slices. Season with salt and pepper.

Drain the tuna from its preserving oil, and mash it roughly with a fork. Add it to the mayonnaise, mix, and test for seasoning. Spread the mayonnaise over the pork slices, then arrange the anchovy fillets on top. Scatter with the capers, and place a few small basil leaves around.

Bollito misto
Boiled duck with chicken and cotechino

For 8-10 This alternative recipe for Bollito Misto requires careful timing, starting individual ingredients cooking at different times so that they "finish" together. You need three large saucepans to hold the ducks, chickens, and cotechino respectively.

3 small ducks, about 3 1/2 pounds each
2 large free-range chickens, about 6 pounds each
3 precooked cotechino or 2 precooked zampone
coarse sea salt and freshly ground black pepper
3 heads celery, hearts and leaves
12 organic carrots, scrubbed and halved lengthways
8 bay leaves
1 bunch fresh thyme
1 head garlic, quartered
1 bunch flat-leaf parsley
1 tablespoon white peppercorns
12 Yukon Gold potatoes, peeled and halved lengthways, or 1 cup cannellini beans or
    lentils, cooked (see page 346)

Fill a saucepan large enough to hold the ducks with enough water to keep the ducks completely submerged. Bring the water to the boil.

Remove the fat from the inside of the ducks, then season the cavities generously. Divide the leafy tops of the celery between the duck cavities, and place in each a halved whole carrot, 2 bay leaves, a sprig of thyme, and a quarter of the garlic. Wrap each duck in a clean towel and then tie securely with string.

2 hours before serving Place the ducks into the boiling water and weight down to keep them submerged. Simmer for 2 hours. Remove, drain well, and cool before unwrapping.

1 hour before serving After cooking the duck for 1 hour, put the chickens into another saucepan large enough to hold them. Add water to cover, as well as 2 celery sticks, 2 halved carrots, the remaining bay leaves and garlic, 3 sprigs of thyme, the parsley stalks, and peppercorns. Bring to the boil, then simmer for about 1 hour.

30 minutes before serving Half an hour after you put the chickens on, place the zampone or cotechino in a separate saucepan and cook according to the instructions on the packet.

20 minutes before serving Add the remaining carrots, the celery hearts cut in quarters, and the potatoes if using to the simmering chickens and stock. Season the stock at this stage. Chop the parsley.

To serve Test the chickens for doneness by pulling a leg away from the body; it should come away easily if cooked. Remove from the pan and drain. Drain the vegetables, discarding the herbs and vegetables from the original stock. Strain and reserve the stock. Heat the cannellini beans or lentils if using.

Cut thick 1/2-in slices from the breast and leg of the ducks, the chickens into similar slices, using both white and dark meat, the cotechino or zampone into 1/2-in slices at an angle.

Arrange all the meats on a large warm serving plate and pour over some of the seasoned chicken stock. Arrange the carrots, celery and potatoes, cannellini beans or lentils around the meats, and scatter everything with parsley. Serve with Salsa di Dragoncello, Salsa di Rafano, and mustard fruits (see pages 309, 304, and 347).

Faraona con latte e maggiorana
Guinea fowl pan-roasted with milk and marjoram

For 6

3 guinea fowl or small free-range chickens
1 bunch fresh marjoram
5 garlic cloves, peeled
coarse sea salt and freshly ground black pepper
1 tablespoon olive oil
1 cup vermouth
1 quart milk
peel of 2 lemons

Preheat the oven to 400° F.

Chop half the marjoram and 2 of the garlic cloves finely. Add the rest of the marjoram leaves, and season with salt and pepper. Add 1 tablespoon olive oil to hold it together.

With your hand gently separate the skin of the guinea fowl from the meat, and push a generous amount of herbs into the pocket between skin and meat of the breasts and legs. Put the rest of the garlic inside the birds. Place in a roasting pan.

Roast the guinea fowl in the preheated oven for 30 minutes, then add the vermouth to the dish, lower the heat to 340° F, and cook for 5 minutes. Add the milk and lemon peel, and cook for another 30 minutes.

Remove the guinea fowl from the oven and dish, and place on a heated plate. Put the roasting pan over a medium heat and bring to a gentle boil, scraping the juices. Let the liquid boil until you have a dark sauce. Pour over the guinea fowl and serve.

Pollo al sale con pancetta
Salt-roasted chicken wrapped in pancetta

For 6

3 small free-range organic chickens, about 2 1/2 pounds each
coarse sea salt and freshly ground black pepper
30 bay leaves, fresh if possible
3 lemons, washed, dried, and pricked all over
1 pound pancetta, thinly sliced
4 1/2 pounds natural coarse sea salt

Preheat the oven to 350° F.

Wash each chicken well inside and out, and dry with paper towels. Season inside and out. Push half a handful of bay leaves into the cavities followed by a lemon. Push a few more bay leaves in with a slice of pancetta. Arrange the remaining pancetta, about 5 slices per bird, over the breasts, and tie to secure.

Place the chickens on their sides, side by side, in a large stainless-steel pan or casserole; they should fit snugly. Cover with the coarse salt, making sure that the salt packs down the sides, fills the spaces between each chicken, and covers the breasts by at least 1/2 in. Cover and put in the oven for 2 hours.

Test for doneness by breaking off a part of the salt crust and inserting the point of a knife into the leg – the juices should be clear and the meat moist but not pink.

Remove all the salt crust from the birds and brush off excess salt. Take the pancetta off the breast, cut the birds in half, and serve one-half per helping, with some of the pancetta and Salsa Verde (see page 311).

Lombo di capriolo con coppa
Loins of venison wrapped in coppa

For 8

1 saddle of venison, the 2 loins taken from the bone, and trimmed of fat and sinew

4 garlic cloves, peeled and thinly sliced

1 bunch fresh rosemary

2 ounces fat from prosciutto di Parma, or bacon fat, cut into slivers (as the garlic)

coarse sea salt and freshly ground black pepper

1 pound coppa di Parma, thinly sliced

2 tablespoons unsalted butter

2 tablespoons olive oil

1 1/2 cups red wine

Preheat the oven to 425° F. Place the loins on a board, and make small incisions along the grain of each, 2 in apart. Into each push a sliver of garlic, a sprig of rosemary, a small piece of prosciutto fat, and some salt and pepper. Both loins should be studded on all sides. Place two pieces of wax paper on the board, and arrange the coppa slices over each, overlapping to form two rectangles that will accommodate the loins. Place the loins in the center and roll up the papers so that each loin is completely wrapped in coppa. Remove the papers carefully. Tie the coppa wrapping in place with string.

Heat the butter and oil in a heavy-bottomed roasting pan and seal the loins on all sides. Add half the red wine and roast for 20 minutes. Turn the loins over and roast for a further 15 minutes. Test for rare by pressing with your finger: it should feel soft and giving. For medium-rare, roast for a further 5 minutes. Remove to a serving platter. Deglaze the pan with the remainder of the red wine. Slice the meat thickly and serve with the pan juices.

Anatra vapore e arrosto
Steamed and roasted duck

For 6

2 ducks, about 3 1/2 pounds each

coarse sea salt and freshly ground black pepper

8 garlic cloves, peeled

3 lemons, halved

4 celery stalks, with their leaves, roughly chopped

4 small carrots, scrubbed and roughly chopped

6 tablespoons balsamic vinegar

2 tablespoons unsalted butter

Preheat the oven to 400° F. Trim the neck skin from the ducks and remove all fat from the cavities. Using a fork, prick the duck skin in places where the fat deposits are thickest. Rub the whole ducks inside and out with sea salt.

Pulse-chop the garlic, 2 of the lemons, the celery stalks and leaves, and the carrots. Add salt and pepper. Push this mixture inside each bird. Squeeze the remaining lemon over the birds, and set them breast side up in a roasting pan on a rack. Half fill the pan with boiling water. Completely cover the ducks with foil, wrapping it round the edge of the pan to make an airtight seal. Steam-bake for 1 hour. Remove the foil, and pour away the water. Pour half of the balsamic vinegar over the ducks and season the breasts. Turn the oven temperature up to 425° F. Roast for a further 15 minutes to brown the breasts, then turn the ducks over. Reduce the oven temperature to 400° F, and roast for a further 45-60 minutes. The skin should be dark brown and crisp, the flesh coming away from the bones.

Rest for 5 minutes before carving. Deglaze the roasting pan with the butter, vinegar, and 1 tablespoon of lemon juice. Pour over each serving of duck and stuffing.

Tetraone marinato nel latte
Roast grouse marinated in milk

For 6

6 grouse
1 quart milk
coarse sea salt and freshly ground black pepper
6 garlic cloves, peeled and crushed with the flat of a knife
1 bunch fresh sage, leaves picked from the stalks
1 bunch fresh rosemary, leaves picked from the stalks
12 ounces pancetta, thinly sliced
4 ounces (1 stick) unsalted butter
zest of 3 lemons
1/2 cup Vin Santo or other sweet wine

Place the milk in a container large enough to hold the birds, add salt and pepper and the garlic. Chop half the sage and rosemary and rub over each bird before placing them in the marinade. Leave for 1-2 hours in a cool place. Preheat the oven to 400° F.

Remove the grouse from the marinade and dry them. Wrap the breast of each bird in the pancetta slices, tying them on with string, and tucking sage leaves between the slices. Put some of the rosemary and a piece of garlic into each cavity. Melt the butter in two heavy-bottomed casseroles, and brown three birds in each on all sides. Add enough of the marinade so that it comes about 3/4 in up the sides of the birds. Add the lemon zest, cover, place the birds in the preheated oven, and pot-roast, turning after 10 minutes, for a total of 20-25 minutes.

Place the birds on a serving platter. Reduce the casserole juices and add the Vin Santo. Check the seasoning and pour over the birds.

Tetraone ripiene con bruschetta
Roast grouse stuffed with bruschetta

For 6

6 grouse
6 slices sourdough bread (see page 277)
2 garlic cloves, peeled
1 large bunch fresh thyme
coarse sea salt and freshly ground black pepper
extra virgin olive oil
12 ounces pancetta, thinly sliced
1/2 cup Chianti Classico

Preheat the oven to 450° F.

Ask the game dealer to leave the livers in the birds. Toast the sourdough bread on both sides, and rub while still warm with the garlic and some of the thyme. Season and drizzle each slice with extra virgin olive oil. Break the slices up into smallish pieces and stuff into the grouse. Place a sprig of thyme inside each bird as well.

Wrap each bird in the pancetta slices, tying them on with string. Heat a roasting pan, then brush lightly with oil. Brown the birds on all sides in the pan, then place in the preheated oven and roast for 20 minutes, a little longer if the birds are larger. Remove from the oven, place on a serving platter, and allow to rest for 5-10 minutes.

Deglaze the roasting pan with the Chianti. Pour this juice over each bird, pulling the bruschetta out from the cavity. Drizzle some extra virgin olive oil over, and serve with arugula or mustard leaves.

Fagiano ripieno di ricotta in tegame
Pot-roasted pheasant stuffed with ricotta

For 6

3 small hen pheasants
coarse sea salt and freshly ground black pepper
1 pound ricotta cheese
1 bunch fresh sage leaves
8 ounces pancetta, very thinly sliced
8 tablespoons (1 stick) unsalted butter
1/2 cup Vecchio Romagna or other dark brandy

Season the cavity of each bird and then fill with the ricotta and a few sage leaves. Lay the thin slices of pancetta over the breasts of each bird, inserting a sage leaf or two as well. Tie round each pheasant with string to secure the pancetta.

Use a thick heavy saucepan or casserole with a lid that the birds will fit into snugly. Put the butter in the pan and melt over a high heat. Brown the pheasants on all sides, then sprinkle with salt and pepper. Add any remaining sage leaves, cover with the lid, and turn the heat to low. Cook for about 45 minutes, turning the birds quite frequently and basting each time.

Remove the pheasants from the saucepan, and keep warm on a serving plate. Add the Vecchio Romagna to the pan and heat quickly, stirring to deglaze.

Remove the string and divide each pheasant into two. Serve with the cooked ricotta and the juices poured over.

Pernice con timo e mascarpone
Roast partridge with thyme and mascarpone

For 6

6 partridges, plucked and cleaned
coarse sea salt and freshly ground black pepper
8 ounces mascarpone cheese
2 tablespoons each of fresh flat-leaf parsley, fresh marjoram, and
    fresh thyme, leaves picked from the stalks and chopped
12 ounces pancetta, thinly sliced
3 tablespoons olive oil
1/3 cup red wine or stock

Preheat the oven to 425° F.

Season the cavities of the partridges with salt and pepper.

In a bowl gently combine the mascarpone with the herbs, then season with salt and pepper. Place a large tablespoon of this mixture inside each partridge. Wrap the pancetta around the partridges and tie on with string.

Heat the olive oil in a roasting pan and brown the birds on all sides. Put in the preheated oven and roast for 15 minutes. Remove from the oven and place the birds on a warm plate while you make the sauce.

Pour out any fat from the pan, then deglaze with the red wine or stock. Add the remaining mascarpone and cook over a high heat for a minute. Pour over the partridges and serve.

Piccione alla griglia marinato con vin santo
Grilled pigeon marinated in vin santo

For 6

6 pigeons
coarse sea salt and coarsely ground black pepper
2 small dried red chiles, crumbled
1/2 head celery, leaves chopped, stalks finely sliced
1 small red onion, peeled and finely chopped
6 garlic cloves, peeled and sliced
1 bunch fresh thyme, leaves picked from the stalks
2 1/4 cups Vin Santo
3 tablespoons olive oil

To flatten the birds, using a large knife, make a cut down either side of the backbone and remove. Now use a small knife and carefully cut the body carcass and breast bones away from the meat. Spread each bird out flat, and place in a large flat dish. Season with salt, pepper, and chile, and scatter over the celery, onion, garlic, and thyme. Add the Vin Santo and olive oil. Cover and marinate for 2-3 hours or overnight in the fridge.

Preheat the grill. Remove the birds from the marinade; strain and keep the liquid. Place the birds on the grill, skin side down, and cook for 3-4 minutes, positioning the legs of each bird, which take longer to cook, on the hottest part of the grill. The breast should remain slightly pink. Turn and cook for a further 5-10 minutes. Spoon a little of the marinade over each bird in the final few minutes. Remove from the grill, and spoon a little more marinade over each bird while they rest.

Piccione in vino rosso
Pigeons braised in red wine

For 6

6 pigeons

2 tablespoons olive oil

1 red onion, peeled and roughly chopped

6 ounces pancetta, cut into matchsticks

5 garlic cloves, peeled and coarsely sliced

1 dried red chile, crumbled

2 ounces dried porcini, soaked for 30 minutes in hot water, drained, and roughly
    chopped

1 tablespoon cumin seeds

1/2 cup red wine

1 1-pound can peeled plum tomatoes, drained of their juices

8 juniper berries

coarse sea salt and freshly ground black pepper

2 tablespoons Dijon mustard

Preheat the oven to 425° F. Use a heavy casserole with a lid. Heat the oil and seal the pigeons on all sides. Remove.

Fry the onion and pancetta in the hot oil and when soft, add the garlic, chile, and mushrooms. After 3 minutes add the cumin, then stir and cook for 5 minutes. Add the wine, tomatoes, and juniper, and bring to the boil. Add the pigeons, breast side down. The liquid should come halfway up each bird. Cover and bake for 2 hours. Stir the mustard into the juices, season, and serve hot or cold.

Bread
Brusch

Pizza

hetta

10

Sourdough bread Pagnotta Pizza Pizza con revisa
e acciughe Pizza con robiola, tartufo bianco, e tuo
patate, taleggio, e tartufo bianco Bruschetta Crost
crude Bruschetta con cavolo nero e olio Bruschetta
Bruschetta con acciughe marinate nel vino Crostin

o, pancetta, e rosmarino   Pizza con mozzarella, trevisano,
a   Pizza con taleggio, carciofi, e prosciutto   Pizza con
   Bruschetta con cannellini freschi   Bruschetta con fave
n erbe secche   Bruschetta con fave secche e peperoncino
egatini di pollo e acciughe

Potato sourdough starter

Makes about 14-16 ounces

2 medium potatoes (10 ounces) peeled and cut into 3/4-in dice
3 3/4 cups plain bread flour
a few grains of active dry yeast (just a mere pinch)

Cook the potatoes in 2 cups unsalted water until soft. Mash with a fork in the water and leave to cool. Add 1 1/3 cups of the flour and yeast and mix thoroughly until you have a batter. Put into a large 2-quart sterile glass jar or pitcher and seal tightly with plastic wrap. Leave in a dark place for 30 hours, until the surface is covered with tiny bubbles. Stir the starter which will have begun to ferment and expand. Recover and leave for 24 hours.

Uncover the starter, add 3/4 cup flour and 1/4 cup lukewarm water. Stir to mix. Cover again and put back in the warm place for 48 hours.

Uncover the starter and put into a warm bowl. Add a further 1 1/3 cups flour and 1/4 cup lukewarm water. Mix together until the flour is incorporated, and then leave covered with plastic wrap to double in volume. It takes about 6 hours before the sourdough is ready for use. Store in a sterile container in the refrigerator, tightly covered.

To keep the sourdough active, you must use it once a week. Replace the amount used with the same amount of flour and water, in equal portions. (For example, if you use 1/2 cup starter, stir 1/4 cup each flour and water into the sourdough container.) If you don't use the starter to make bread, you must "feed" it. Discard at least 1/2 cup starter every week, replacing it with 1/4 cup each flour and water.

Sourdough bread

Makes 2 loaves Use this bread for bruschetta.

1 2/3 cups Potato Sourdough Starter (see previous recipe and page 347)
8 cups plain unbleached flour
2 1/2 cups lukewarm water
4 teaspoons sea salt
4 tablespoons olive oil

In a heavy-duty mixer fitted with a paddle, mix the starter with the 4 cups flour and half the water for about 8 minutes on slow speed. Remove, cover with plastic wrap, and leave in a warm place for 30 minutes. Add the remaining water, the salt, and olive oil, and stir in enough flour to make a stiff dough. Return to the machine, and knead with the dough hook for a further 5 minutes—you should have a wet dough. Remove, place in a lightly oiled bowl, cover with plastic wrap, and leave to double in volume in a warm place, about 2 1/2 hours.

Place the dough on a floured surface and divide into two. Knead each piece roughly into a round loaf. Place each loaf on a cornmeal-dusted baking sheet. Cover with damp cloths and let stand until almost doubled, about 1 1/2 hours.

Preheat the oven to 450° F.

Make a cut across each loaf. Place in the preheated oven after spraying the inside of the oven with water, using a spray bottle. Bake for 10 minutes, then check for browning. Turn if necessary. Spray the oven again, and reduce the heat to 400°. Continue baking for a further 20-30 minutes. Turn the loaves around after 20 minutes. The bread is cooked when it sounds hollow after tapping. Cool on wire racks.

Pagnotta

Makes 1 large loaf Pagnotta is semolina sourdough bread made in Puglia. Use it for bruschetta.

Sponge

2 1/2 cups (80° F) water

1/2 cup (4 ounces) Potato Sourdough Starter (see page 276)

1/4 teaspoon active dry yeast

2 1/3 cups unbleached flour

Bread

1 cup plus 2 tablespoons (80° F) water

4 teaspoons fine sea salt

1/4 teaspoon active dry yeast

6 to 7 cups durum semolina (pasta flour)

3/4 cup whole wheat flour

Sponge Fill the mixing bowl of a standing heavy-duty mixer with warm tap water, let stand until warm, then discard the water and dry the bowl. Add the 2 1/2 cups water, starter, and yeast and mix to dissolve the starter. Add the flour and stir well until smooth. Cover with plastic wrap and let stand overnight in a warm (around 80° F), draft-free place. It will be covered with tiny bubbles.

Bread Stir the water, salt, and yeast into the sponge. Attach the bowl to the mixer. Using the paddle blade on low speed, mix in 3 cups of the semolina to make a thick batter. Add the whole wheat flour. Gradually mix in enough of the remaining flour to make a somewhat soft, slightly sticky dough. Change to the dough hook, and knead the dough until smooth, about 10 minutes. Transfer to a floured work surface and knead briefly to check the dough's texture (it should be elastic and moist, but not sticky).

Form the dough into a large bowl. Place on a large nonstick baking sheet (or a baking sheet lined with a double thickness of parchment paper). Loosely cover with large sheets of plastic wrap. Let stand in a warm (80° F), draft-free place until almost doubled in bulk, 5 to 6 hours.

Preheat the oven to 450° F. Remove the plastic wrap. Using a sharp knife, cut a large, shallow "X" in the top of the loaf. Bake for 20 minutes. Reduce the oven temperature to 350° F, and bake until the loaf is dark golden brown and the bottom sounds hollow when tapped. Cool completely on a wire rack.

Pizza dough

For 6, making 10-inch pizzas We use the basic pizza dough recipe from Alice Waters' Chez Panisse restaurant in Berkeley, California.

Step 1
4 teaspoons active dry yeast
1/2 cup warm (100° to 110° F) water
1 cup rye flour
Step 2
1 cup warm (100° to 110° F) water
2 tablespoons milk
1/4 cup extra-virgin olive oil
1 1/4 teaspoon fine sea salt
3 1/2 cups unbleached flour

Fill a heavy-duty mixing bowl with hot water; pour out water and dry.

Mix the yeast with the 1/2 cup warm water in the warm bowl; stir to dissolve. Stir in the rye flour to make a stiff dough. Cover and leave in a warm place until puffy, about 1 hour.

Add the remaining ingredients. Attach the bowl to the mixer fitted with a paddle, and mix into a soft dough. Change to the dough hook, and knead for 10-15 minutes. The dough will be quite wet and sticky (this texture will make a crisper crust).

Place the dough in a bowl greased with extra olive oil, and turn to grease the top. Cover with plastic wrap and leave to rise in a warm place until doubled, about 1 1/2 hours. Knock the dough back, and knead a couple of times then return to the bowl and let it rise until almost doubled, about 40 minutes.

Preheat the oven to 450° F, and have ready a large flat baking tray or a pizza stone.

When the dough is ready, divide into six pieces, and individually form into balls. Roll out each ball on a floured surface with quick light motions as thinly as possible. A dough should roll out to make a 10-inch pizza base.

Pizza con trevisano, pancetta, e rosmarino
Pizza with Treviso radicchio, pancetta, and rosemary

6 10-in pizza bases (see page 280)
3 heads Treviso radicchio
extra virgin olive oil
fresh mozzarella, thinly sliced
2 branches fresh rosemary, leaves picked from the stalks, finely chopped
coarse sea salt and freshly ground black pepper
6 ounces pancetta, thinly sliced

Pull the leaves from the thick white stalks of the radicchio, and shred them. Wash thoroughly, and drain well. Toss with 3 tablespoons olive oil. Place the radicchio on the pizza bases, followed by the sliced mozzarella, and scatter with rosemary, salt, and pepper. Place the slices of pancetta over the top, about four per pizza. Drizzle lightly with a little more olive oil and bake in the preheated oven until the cheese has melted, the pancetta is cooked, and the crust is crisp, about 6-8 minutes.

Pizza con mozzarella, trevisano, e acciughe
Pizza with mozzarella, Treviso radicchio, and anchovies

6 10-in pizza bases (see page 280)
18 salted anchovy fillets, prepared (see page 346)
coarsely ground black pepper
2 lemons
1/2 cup olive oil
2 branches fresh rosemary, leaves picked from the stalks, finely chopped
3 medium or 2 large heads Treviso radicchio
fresh mozzarella, thinly sliced

Place the anchovy fillets in a dish. Sprinkle them with a little black pepper, the zest and juice of one of the lemons, and half the olive oil. Sprinkle the chopped rosemary over the fillets, and leave to marinate for a few minutes.

Remove the flimsy torn outer leaves of the radicchio heads, and peel the stalks. Cut each head in half lengthways, then in half again if they are medium, into eighths if large. Toss with the remaining oil and lemon juice.

Scatter the radicchio over the pizza bases, and place the mozzarella slices on top. Arrange the marinated anchovy fillets over the mozzarella, then bake in the preheated oven for 6-8 minutes until the dough is cooked. The mozzarella should just be melted, and the pizza crust crisp.

Pizza con robiola, tartufo bianco, e rucola
Pizza with robiola, white truffle, and arugula

Robiola is an unpasteurized, unpressed, cows' milk cheese.

6 10-in pizza bases (see page 280)
4 1/2 ounces Robiola cheese, cut into pieces
coarse sea salt and freshly ground black pepper
1/4 cup extra virgin olive oil
1 bunch arugula
juice of 1/2 lemon
1/2 cup white truffle oil

Scatter the pieces of Robiola over the pizzas, then season with salt and pepper. Drizzle half the extra virgin olive oil over the pizzas and bake in the preheated oven until the dough is cooked.

Meanwhile, dress the arugula with the remaining extra virgin olive oil and the lemon juice.

Remove the pizzas from the oven. Drizzle the truffle oil over the melted Robiola and scatter with some dressed arugula.

Pizza con taleggio, carciofi, e prosciutto
Pizza with taleggio, artichokes, and prosciutto

6 10-in pizza bases (see page 280)

6 small artichokes, prepared (see page 172)

2 tablespoons extra virgin olive oil

coarse sea salt and freshly ground black pepper

2 garlic cloves, peeled and finely chopped

1 bunch thyme, leaves picked from the stalks

12 ounces Taleggio cheese, roughly cut, rind removed

10 ounces prosciutto, thinly sliced

In a heavy-bottomed pan, heat the olive oil, add the artichoke hearts, and season with salt and pepper, garlic, and thyme. Cook the hearts, turning them continuously so they don't burn, for about 10 minutes. Remove from the pan and cool.

Dot the pieces of Taleggio over the pizza bases. Scatter the slices of artichoke heart over the Taleggio, then season with salt and pepper. Bake in the preheated oven until the dough is cooked. When ready, serve with a slice of prosciutto laid over the top of the pizza.

Pizza con patate, taleggio, e tartufo bianco
Pizza with potato, taleggio, and white truffle

6 10-in pizza bases (see page 280)
1 pound Yukon Gold or other yellow potatoes, scrubbed clean
10 ounces Taleggio cheese, cut into thin slices, rind removed
coarse sea salt and freshly ground black pepper
1/2 cup olive oil
2 ounces white truffle, carefully brushed clean

Slice the potatoes on the finest setting of the mandoline; they should be transparent. Leave in a bowl of cold water to remove the starch, then drain and pat dry.

Place the Taleggio over the pizza bases, and cover with the slices of potato. Season with salt and pepper, drizzle with oil, and bake in the preheated oven until the dough is crisp, about 6-8 minutes. Shave the truffle abundantly over the pizzas.

Alternatively, you can scatter the cooked pizzas with 7 ounces Parmesan shavings and drizzle with 6 tablespoons white truffle oil.

Bruschetta

For 6

6 slices pugliese or sourdough bread, cut 1/2 in thick
1 large garlic clove, peeled
extra virgin olive oil

Toast the bread on both sides then lightly rub with the garlic. Drizzle with extra virgin olive oil then serve with your chosen topping.

Crostini

For 6

6 slices ciabatta bread, cut at an angle, 1/2 in thick
1 large garlic clove, peeled
extra virgin olive oil

Toast the bread on both sides then lightly rub with the garlic. Drizzle with extra virgin olive oil and serve with your chosen topping.

Bruschetta con cannellini freschi
Tomato bruschetta with fresh cannellini

For 6 The season for fresh cannellini beans is short, from August to September.

6 slices pugliese bruschetta (see page 290)

3 large ripe sweet tomatoes, halved

3 teaspoons dried wild oregano

3 small dried red chiles, crumbled

6 tablespoons extra virgin olive oil

Cannellini beans

3 pounds fresh cannellini beans in their shells

3 large garlic cloves, peeled

1 bunch fresh sage

2 large ripe sweet tomatoes

coarse sea salt and freshly ground black pepper

Shell the beans, then place in a heavy-bottomed saucepan. Cover with water, and add the garlic, sage, and tomatoes. Bring to the boil, then turn the heat down, and gently simmer for 30-60 minutes according to freshness. They must not become mushy. Drain, remove the sage, garlic, and any bits of tomato skin and stalk. Season with salt, pepper, and olive oil.

Squash one half tomato onto each bruschetta, then sprinkle with some of the oregano and chile. Drizzle with olive oil, then add a ladleful of warm cannellini beans to cover half of each bruschetta. Serve immediately.

Bruschetta con fave crude
Bruschetta with mashed fava beans

For 6

3 pounds young fava beans, shelled weight
2 garlic cloves, peeled
1/4 cup fresh mint leaves
1/4 cup freshly grated Pecorino cheese
1/4 cup olive oil
coarse sea salt and freshly ground black pepper
juice of 1 lemon
6 slices sourdough bruschetta (see page 290)

Pound the fava beans in a pestle and mortar with the garlic and mint. When the mixture is thick in texture, remove and place in a bowl. Stir in the Pecorino and the olive oil. Season with salt and pepper and the lemon juice and serve on the bruschetta.

Bruschetta con cavolo nero e olio
Bruschetta with cavolo nero and oil

For 6

12 leaves kale or cavolo nero, washed and hard stalks removed
1 quart Vegetable Stock (see page 143) or water
coarse sea salt and freshly ground black pepper
6 slices pugliese bruschetta (see page 290)
extra virgin olive oil

Bring the stock or salted water to a boil. Add the cavolo, lower the heat, and simmer for 10 minutes or until soft. Put 2 pieces on top of each bruschetta. Pour on some oil, and season.

Bruschetta con erbe secche
Bruschetta with dried herbs

For 6

1 tablespoon each of dried oregano, thyme, and marjoram (or one or two herbs)
1 teaspoon fennel seeds
6 slices sourdough bruschetta (see page 290)
3 dried red chiles, crumbled
coarse sea salt and freshly ground black pepper
extra virgin olive oil

Scatter the herbs and seeds lightly over each bruschetta, then cautiously add the chile, salt, and pepper. Drizzle over extra virgin olive oil, and serve immediately.

Bruschetta con fave secche e peperoncino
Bruschetta with dried fava beans and chile

For 6

2 1/2 cups dried and peeled fava beans
1 celery stalk
2 bay leaves
2 garlic cloves, peeled
1/4 cup extra virgin olive oil
4 small fresh hot red chiles
coarse sea salt and freshly ground black pepper
6 slices pugliese bruschetta (see page 290)

Soak the beans in cold water overnight. When ready to cook, preheat the oven to 350° F.

Drain the beans and place in an earthenware pot with a lid. Cover with water to twice the depth of the beans, and add the celery, bay, and garlic. Cover and bake for 2 hours or until the water has been absorbed. The beans should be so soft that you can smash them to a pulp with a wooden spoon.

In a small pan heat the olive oil, and fry the whole chiles for a minute to allow them to cook and turn from red to red-brown. Add the whole fried chiles to your mashed beans, smashing them into the purée to break them up. Season and serve on the bruschetta.

Bruschetta con acciughe marinate nel vino
Bruschetta with anchovies marinated in wine

For 6

18 salted anchovies, washed
1/4 cup Chardonnay wine
freshly ground black pepper
1 dried red chile, crumbled
zest and juice of 2 lemons
1/2 cup extra virgin olive oil
3 tablespoons finely chopped parsley
a handful of bitter leaves, blanched in boiling water (see method)
3 lemons, quartered
6 thick slices sourdough bruschetta (see page 290)

Place the anchovies in a bowl and cover with wine. Leave to marinate for 2 hours or overnight. Fillet each anchovy, lay out on a flat dish, and season with black pepper, crushed dried chile and lemon zest. Drizzle over the olive oil and a few drops of the lemon juice. Scatter generously with parsley.

Serve the anchovies with blanched bitter greens such as cicoria, broccoli rabe, kale or cavolo nero, or Swiss chard, the bruschetta, and lemon quarters.

Crostini di fegatini di pollo e acciughe
Crostini of chicken livers with anchovies

1 pound chicken livers

1 tablespoon olive oil

1 cup dry vermouth

6 salted anchovy fillets, prepared (see page 346)

2 teaspoons salted capers, prepared (see page 346)

1 cup Chicken Stock (see page 142)

coarse sea salt and freshly ground black pepper

2 to 3 tablespoons unsalted butter

6 crostini (see page 290)

Remove any sinew and skin from the chicken livers, then wash and dry.

Heat the oil in a saucepan. Add the livers and cook for several minutes until brown, adding the vermouth from time to time, and scraping the juices from the bottom of the pan. Remove from the pan to a board and chop with a mezzaluna or knife until coarse. Return to the pan.

Chop the anchovies and capers until of the same consistency as the livers, then add to the livers. Cook for 10 minutes, adding several tablespoons of stock from time to time, to achieve a creamy consistency. Add salt and pepper and stir in the butter with a fork.

Put the livers on top of each crostini and serve.

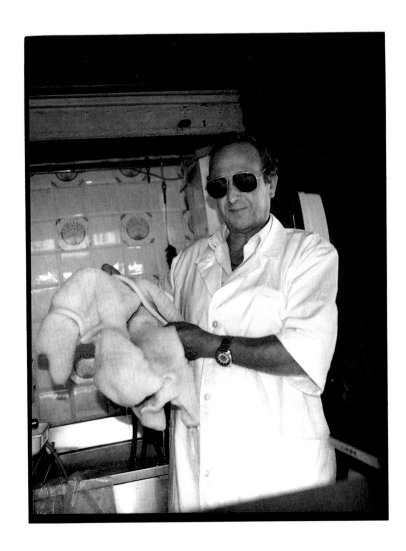

Salsa di rafano   Pomodoro concentrato   Salsa di ca
finocchio   Salsa di aceto balsamico   Salsa di basil
rosmarino   Salsa calda d'acciughe   Salsa di dragonce
basilico   Maionese con acciughe   Salsa verde

nella   Salsa di peperoncino verde   Salsa di pimento e
o e olive   Salsa di erbetta verde   Salsa d'acciughe e
lo   Salmoriglio   Maionese di olio nuovo   Maionese con

Salsa di rafano
Fresh horseradish

Serve with boiled meats.

6-ounce piece fresh horseradish, peeled
1 loaf ciabatta bread
1/4 cup red wine vinegar
2 garlic cloves, peeled and finely chopped
2/3 cup olive oil
coarse sea salt and freshly ground black
    pepper

Remove and discard the crust from the bread. Tear the bread into small pieces, then pulse-chop in the food processor to coarse bread crumbs.

Place the bread crumbs in a bowl, then add the vinegar and enough water to moisten the bread crumbs. Put aside for 10 minutes before squeezing as dry as possible.

Grate the horseradish finely on the cheese grater. Combine with the garlic and squeezed bread crumbs, then slowly add the olive oil, stirring continuously as for mayonnaise. Season with salt and pepper.

Pomodoro concentrato
Tomato and chile paste

This is good with salt cod, or grilled eggplants.

1 28-ounce can peeled plum tomatoes
1 tablespoon olive oil
2 garlic cloves, peeled and chopped
1 small red onion, peeled and finely
    chopped
3 red chiles, seeded and finely chopped
coarse sea salt and freshly ground black
    pepper

In a heavy saucepan heat the oil and add the garlic, onion, and chile. Cook for 15 minutes over a low heat until very soft but not brown. Drain off some of the olive oil.

Return the pan to the heat, and add the drained tomatoes with a little juice. Cook over a low heat for 1 1/2 hours, when the sauce should be very thick and any remaining oil has risen to the top. Stir frequently throughout cooking to prevent the sauce from sticking. Season to taste.

Pour onto a flat plate and leave to cool. Serve in spoonfuls.

Salsa di cannella
Tomato and cinnamon

Serve with grilled lamb or grilled eggplant.

2 28-ounce cans plum tomatoes, drained
    of most of their juices
1/4 cup olive oil
4 garlic cloves, peeled and thinly sliced
3 teaspoons coriander seeds, crushed
1-2 dried red chiles, crumbled
2 whole cinnamon sticks
coarse sea salt and freshly ground black
    pepper

Heat the oil in a pan and gently fry the garlic, coriander seeds, chile, and cinnamon. When the garlic is golden brown, add the tomatoes and roughly break them up. Season with salt and pepper, and cook slowly, stirring occasionally, for at least 1 1/2 hours. Taste again for seasoning. The sauce should be thick and sweet with a hint of the chile, coriander, and cinnamon. Remove the cinnamon sticks before serving.

Salsa di peperoncino verde
Green chile and lemon peel

This sauce is good with scallops, squid, or grilled fish.

6 hot green chiles
1 lemon
coarse sea salt and freshly ground black
    pepper
1/2 cup extra virgin olive oil

Seed and finely chop the chiles.

Cut the peel off the lemon (making sure there is no white pith), and slice into very fine strips. Combine with the chopped chile. Add salt and pepper, and mix with the olive oil. Let sit for several hours before serving.

Salsa di pimento e finocchio
Fresh red chile and fennel

Serve with grilled or roasted fish, or crab salad.

6 fresh chiles, seeded and finely chopped
2 ounces fresh green fennel herb or fennel
    bulb tops, chopped
1/2 garlic clove, peeled and finely chopped
    (optional)
coarse sea salt and freshly ground black
    pepper
1/2 cup extra virgin olive oil
juice of 2 lemons

Combine the chile, fennel, garlic if
using, and seasoning. Cover with the
olive oil and finally add the lemon juice.

Salsa di aceto balsamico
Balsamic red peppercorn

This is good with grilled fish or grilled lamb.

2 garlic cloves, peeled
3 tablespoons red peppercorns
coarse sea salt and freshly ground black
    pepper
2 medium fresh red chiles, seeded and
    chopped
6 tablespoons balsamic vinegar
2/3 cup extra virgin olive oil
juice of 2 lemons
3 tablespoons chopped fresh flat-leaf
    parsley

Pound the garlic and peppercorns
together in a pestle and mortar with a
little salt.

When they are well crushed, add the
chile, balsamic vinegar, olive oil, and
lemon juice. Stir in the parsley, and
season with salt and pepper.

Salsa di basilico e olive
Basil, olive, and anchovy

We serve this sauce with grilled turbot or roasted turbot tranche (see page 230).

9 ounces small black Niçoise olives, pitted
6 salted anchovies, prepared (see page 346)
1 garlic clove, peeled and finely chopped
juice of 1 lemon
3 tablespoons balsamic or red wine (Volpaia "Erbe") herb vinegar
1/2 cup extra virgin olive oil
1/4 cup roughly chopped fresh basil leaves
coarse sea salt and freshly ground black pepper

Roughly chop the olives and put in a bowl. Finely chop the anchovy fillets and add to the olives, along with the garlic. Stir in the lemon juice, vinegar, and olive oil, then leave to marinate for 30 minutes before using.

Stir in the basil leaves and adjust the seasoning just before serving.

Salsa di erbetta verde
Green herb and pine nut

2 slices ciabatta bread, bottom crust removed
1 cup pine nuts, lightly toasted
6 tablespoons fresh basil leaves, picked from the stalks, roughly chopped
3 tablespoons roughly chopped fresh flat-leaf parsley
3 tablespoons roughly chopped fresh mint leaves
1/4 cup salted capers, prepared (see page 346)
2 tablespoons white wine vinegar
5 tablespoons extra virgin olive oil
1 teaspoon coarse sea salt
freshly ground black pepper

Tear the ciabatta into pieces and roughly pulse-chop to coarse bread crumbs.

Using a pestle and mortar, lightly pound the pine nuts, then stir in the herbs. Add the bread crumbs and capers, and mix together with the vinegar and olive oil. Season with salt and pepper.

Salsa d'acciughe e rosmarino
Anchovy and rosemary

2 tablespoons finely chopped fresh
    rosemary
12 salted anchovy fillets, prepared (see
    page 346)
juice of 2 lemons
1/2 cup extra virgin olive oil

Crush the rosemary in a mortar, add the anchovies, and pound to a paste. Slowly add the lemon juice, stirring to blend. Finally add the olive oil a drop at a time. When about half has been added, pour in the remainder in a thin, steady stream, stirring continuously. Alternatively, you can use a food processor although this method produces a thicker sauce. Put the rosemary in and chop very finely, then add the anchovy and chop to a thick, fine paste. Pour the oil in slowly. Finally, add the lemon juice.

Salsa calda d'acciughe
Warm anchovy

12 anchovies, salted preferably, prepared
    (see page 346)
3 garlic cloves, peeled
1/2 cup milk
4 tablespoons herb wine vinegar (Volpaia
    "Erbe")
freshly ground black pepper
1/2 cup olive oil

Gently simmer the garlic cloves in the milk until soft, about 15 minutes. Allow to cool.

Put the anchovies in a food processor and pulse-chop to a coarse texture. Add the soft garlic and a little of the milk, and pulse together to form a thick creamy consistency. Add the vinegar and black pepper.

Put this thick sauce into a small saucepan and gently heat. Slowly add the olive oil, stirring all the time. Serve hot.

Salsa di dragoncello
Tarragon

1/2 ciabatta loaf

1/3 cup red wine vinegar

the yolks of 2 hard-boiled eggs

4 ounces fresh tarragon, stalks removed,
    chopped

10 salted anchovy fillets, prepared (see
    page 346), chopped

1/4 cup salted capers, prepared (see
    page 346), chopped

1/2-3/4 cup extra virgin olive oil

Tear the bread into small pieces, and soak in the vinegar for 20 minutes. Remove, squeeze dry, and chop, ideally with a mezzaluna or a knife.

Mash the egg yolks with a fork.

Very gently combine the bread, tarragon, anchovies, capers, and egg in a bowl. Stir in the oil.

Salmoriglio
Summer thyme

Make in the summer, when lemon thyme has lush leaves, or use yellow thyme or large leaf thyme. Serve with vegetables, fish, chicken, carpaccio etc.

3 bunches fresh thyme, washed and
    spun dry

1 garlic clove, peeled

1 tablespoon coarse sea salt

juice of 1 1/2 lemons

5 tablespoons extra virgin olive oil

freshly ground black pepper

Pick the thyme leaves from the stalks, and put them in a mortar with the garlic clove and salt. Crush until you get a fine green paste. Stir in the lemon juice to lubricate, then slowly add the olive oil. Test for seasoning, adding a little pepper. This has a strong salty taste to highlight the perfume of the thyme.

Maionese di olio nuovo
New olive oil mayonnaise

New olive oil has a special pungency in its first few months (November to the end of March).

2 medium egg yolks from very fresh organic
    eggs
2 1/4 cups new season extra virgin olive oil
juice of 1 fresh lemon
coarse sea salt and coarsely ground black
    pepper

Use a pestle and mortar to make the mayonnaise.

Gently stir the yolks with the pestle and combine for a minute. Start adding the new oil drop by drop. Continue until the emulsion is very thick and sticky. At that point add a little lemon juice. Carry on adding oil and lemon juice until you have finished both and have a perfect thick, bright green mayonnaise. Season with salt and pepper.

Maionese con basilico
Basil mayonnaise

Extra virgin olive oil in the summer has lost its peppery quality and is ideal for making basil mayonnaise.

1 recipe New Olive Oil Mayonnaise, as left,
    using extra virgin olive oil
6 tablespoons basil leaves, stalks removed
2 garlic cloves, crushed with a little coarse
    sea salt

Make the mayonnaise as left. Crush the basil leaves in a pestle and mortar with the garlic and salt to form a wet purée. Add to the mayonnaise at the end.

Maionese con acciughe
Anchovy-caper mayonnaise

2 medium egg yolks from very fresh organic
 eggs
2 1/4 cups extra virgin olive oil
juice of 2 lemons
coarse sea salt and coarsely ground black
 pepper
10 salted anchovy fillets, prepared (see
 page 346), roughly chopped
4 tablespoons salted capers, prepared (see
 page 346), roughly chopped
2 tablespoons finely chopped fresh flat-leaf
 parsley

Make the mayonnaise as in New Olive
Oil Mayonnaise left, using the juice of
one of the lemons only. Mix the juice of
the second lemon with the anchovies
and stir into the mayonnaise, then stir
in the capers and parsley.

Salsa verde
Green sauce

1 large bunch fresh flat-leaf parsley, leaves
 picked from the stalks
1 bunch fresh basil, leaves picked from the
 stalks
a handful of fresh mint leaves
3 garlic cloves, peeled
1/2 cup salted capers, prepared (see
 page 346)
6 salted anchovy fillets, prepared (see page
 346)
2 tablespoons red wine vinegar
5 tablespoons extra virgin olive oil
1 tablespoon Dijon mustard
coarse sea salt and freshly ground black
 pepper

If using a food processor, pulse-chop
the parsley, basil, mint, garlic, capers,
and anchovies until roughly blended.
Transfer to a large bowl and add the
vinegar. Slowly pour in the olive oil,
stirring constantly, and finally add the
mustard. Check for seasoning.

This sauce may also be prepared by
hand, on a board, preferably using a
mezzaluna.

Cream T

Fruit Ice

Tortes

e Cream

12

Panna cotta con grappa e lamponi   Panna cotta a car
cioccolato amaro e nocciole arrostite   Torta di mandorl
valpolicella   Bruschetta di albicocche, peschenoci, e su
Gelato alle prugne   Gelato al limone e ricotta   Gelato
Granita al limone   Granita al caffè   Granita alla melagr

amello   Crema di mascarpone   Monte bianco   Torta di
e   Torta di mandorle, limone, e ricotta   Dolce estivo con
sine   Pere al forno con valpolicella   Gelato al ribes nero
con vin santo   Gelato alla nocciola   Sorbetto alla pesc
ana   Tartufi di cioccolato amaro

Panna cotta con grappa e lamponi
Panna cotta with grappa and raspberries

For 8

5 cups heavy cream
2 vanilla beans, split lengthwise
thinly pared zest of 2 lemons
4 teaspoons unflavored gelatin
2/3 cup cold milk
1 cup powdered sugar
1/2 cup grappa, plus extra to serve
1 1/2 pints raspberries

Pour 3 3/4 cups of the cream into a saucepan, add the vanilla beans and lemon zest, bring to the boil, then simmer until reduced by one-third. Remove the cooked lemon zest and keep to one side. Remove the vanilla beans and scrape the softened insides into the cream.

Sprinkle the gelatin over the milk in a small saucepan and soak until softened, about 5 minutes. Stir over low heat until the gelatin dissolves completely. Stir into the hot cream. Cool completely at room temperature. Strain into another bowl.

Whip the remaining 1 1/4 cups cream with the powdered sugar until it holds its shape, fold into the cooled cooked cream, and add the grappa. Place a piece of cooked lemon zest in each of the eight (6 fl ounces) custard cups, and pour in the cream mixture. Cover and allow to set in the fridge for at least 2 hours.

Run a knife inside each cup, then turn out on to dessert plates and serve with fresh raspberries and a tablespoon of grappa poured over the top.

Panna cotta a caramello
Panna cotta with caramel

For 8

5 cups heavy cream

2 vanilla beans, split lengthwise

4-6 pieces thinly pared orange zest

4 teaspoons unflavored gelatin

2/3 cup cold milk

1 cup powdered sugar

1/2 cup Vecchio Romagna (brandy), plus extra to serve

Caramel

1 cup plus 2 tablespoons superfine sugar

3/4 cup water

1 2-inch cinnamon stick

4 ounces freshly squeezed orange juice, heated

To make the caramel, place the sugar, water, and cinnamon in a heavy-bottomed saucepan. Slowly bring to the boil to melt the sugar, then boil to reduce to a thick dark caramel. Remove the cinnamon, then stir in the orange juice. Wet 10-ounce custard bowls, then divide the caramel between them. Cool completely.

Make the basic Panna Cotta as in the previous recipe, substituting orange zest for the lemon zest, and Vecchio Romagna for the grappa. Pour into the dishes on top of the caramel, then cover and allow to set in the refrigerator for at least 2 hours.

Turn out on to dessert plates, and serve with a little Vecchio Romagna over the top.

Crema di mascarpone
Mascarpone cream

For 6 At La Vecchia Osteria near Follonica, this is served as a dessert with cantuccini biscuits. It is also delicious with summer fruits and berries.

1 pound mascarpone cheese
3 organic egg yolks
2/3 cup powdered sugar

Beat the mascarpone lightly. In a separate bowl, beat the egg yolks. Add the sugar to the egg yolks, then fold into the mascarpone. Keep cool until you serve.

Monte bianco

For 6

1 pound fresh chestnuts
1 quart milk
2/3 cup superfine sugar
2 vanilla beans, split open and seeds loosened
8 ounces crème fraîche
a little good-quality bittersweet chocolate

Bring a large saucepan of water to the boil.

Using a small sharp knife, score the fresh chestnuts across the round sides of their outer shells. Drop them into the boiling water and boil for 15-20 minutes according to size. Remove a few chestnuts at a time to shell them; the shell will come off easily so long as the chestnuts are kept hot in the cooking water. Squeeze each chestnut to crack the shell open, then pry the nuts out of the shell. Remove the bitter inner skin.

Heat the milk in a large pan, add the sugar, split vanilla beans, and the shelled and skinned chestnuts, and simmer gently for 40 minutes until the chestnuts become quite soft; the liquid will have reduced.

Put the cooked chestnuts through the coarse blade of a food mill. Add enough of the remaining reduced milk to bring the mixture together to form a thick dough. Test for sweetness.

Using a small plain nozzle, pipe the chestnut dough out into a mountain shape on a flat serving platter; this will take some time! Serve with crème fraîche with some bitter chocolate grated on top.

Torta di cioccolato amaro e nocciole arrostite
Bitter chocolate roasted hazelnut torte

For 12

8 ounces hazelnuts
7 ounces high-quality bittersweet chocolate
8 ounces (2 sticks) unsalted butter, softened
1 cup plus 2 tablespoons superfine sugar
5 large organic eggs

Preheat the oven to 350° F. Butter a 10 x 3-inch springform pan.

Roast the hazelnuts in the preheated oven until their skins become crisp and the nuts begin to color, about 15 minutes. Place the hot nuts in a towel, fold over and rub on a flat surface in the towel. This removes most of the skins. Place the skinned nuts in a food processor and pulse-chop to a rough texture, not a fine flour. Set aside.

Break the chocolate into small pieces and melt in a bowl over a saucepan of simmering water. Cool to tepid. Using an electric mixer, beat the soft butter with the sugar until light and fluffy. Slowly add the melted chocolate, allowing it to blend in. Stir in eggs one by one. Stir in the crushed nuts.

Pour the mixture into the prepared pan, and bake for 40 to 50 minutes. Test for doneness with a skewer—it should come out dry. Turn off the oven, but leave the torte in it, with the door slightly ajar, for a further 30 minutes. Remove the sides of the pan when completely cool.

Torta di mandorle
Almond tart

For 10-12

1 1/2 cups all-purpose flour

a pinch of salt

11 tablespoons (1 stick plus 3 tablespoons) unsalted cold butter, cut into cubes

1/2 cup powdered sugar

2 large organic egg yolks

Filling

1 cup (2 sticks) unsalted butter, softened

1 cup plus 2 tablespoons superfine sugar

8 ounces (1 1/2 cups) blanched whole almonds

3 large organic eggs

For the pastry, pulse the flour, salt, and butter in a food processor until the mixture resembles coarse bread crumbs. Add the sugar, then egg yolks and pulse until the mixture begins to form clumps. Remove, flatten into a disk, wrap in plastic wrap, and chill for at least an hour until very firm.

Preheat the oven to 350° F. Coarsely grate the pastry into a 12-inch loose-bottomed tart pan, then press it evenly on to the sides and bottom. Line the pastry with aluminum foil, then dried beans. Bake for 10 minutes, remove foil and beans. Bake until very light brown, 10 minutes more. Cool. Reduce the temperature to 300° F.

For the filling, cream the butter and sugar until the mixture is pale and light. In a food processor, chop the almonds until fine. Add the butter and sugar and blend, then add the eggs one by one. Spread into the pastry and bake for 45 to 50 minutes, until top is golden brown. Cool and cover with seasonal fruits.

Torta di mandorle, limone e ricotta
Almond, lemon, and ricotta cake

Makes 10-12 servings

2 1/2 cups (9 ounces) sliced, blanched almonds

1/2 cup all-purpose flour

1/3 cup fresh lemon juice (3 lemons)

3 tablespoons finely grated lemon zest (7 lemons)

1 cup (2 sticks) unsalted butter, softened

1 cup plus 2 tablespoons superfine sugar

6 large organic eggs, separated

1 1/4 cups (10 ounces) fresh ricotta cheese

Preheat the oven to 300° F. Butter a 10-inch springform round cake pan, and line with waxed paper.

Coarsely chop the almonds in a food processor. Combine with the flour and lemon zest. Beat the butter and sugar together in a mixer until pale and light. Add the egg yolks one by one, then add the almond mixture.

Put the ricotta in a bowl and lightly beat with a fork. Add the lemon juice. In another bowl, beat the egg whites until they form soft peaks. Fold the egg whites into the almond mixture and finally stir in the ricotta.

Spoon the mixture into the prepared pan and bake in the preheated oven for about 40 minutes until lightly browned. Test by inserting a skewer in the center, which should come out clean. Cool for 10 minutes. Carefully invert onto a plate, remove waxed paper. Turn right side up, and cool on a cake rack.

Dolce estivo con valpolicella
Summer pudding with valpolicella

For 8

1 sourdough loaf, crust removed and cut into 1/2-in slices (see page 277)

1 1/2 pounds black currants (or small strawberries), stalks and leaves removed

1 1/2 pounds red currants, stalks and leaves removed

1 1/2 pounds raspberries (or blackberries)

1 1/2 cups superfine sugar

6 tablespoons water

1 bottle Valpolicella Classico

3 vanilla beans, split lengthways

juice of 1 lemon

Wash the fruit and shake dry. Dissolve the sugar in the water in a heavy-bottomed pan, then boil until the syrup begins to color a light caramel. Remove from the heat, carefully add the Valpolicella, and stir.

Add 1 pound of each fruit plus the vanilla beans to the hot syrup, and return to the stove. Heat gently, stirring, until the fruits begin to release their juices. Try not to break the fruit up. Remove from the heat. Add the lemon juice and uncooked fruit.

Line a 10-in bowl with the bread, so that there are no gaps. Keep aside enough slices to cover the top. Pour the fruit mixture into the bowl; it should easily come to the top, the juices soaking into the bread. Cover with a layer of bread slices, pushing them into the fruit to soak up the juice. Weight down with a small plate that just fits into the bowl. Put in the fridge for at least 4 hours.

Turn out and serve with a few fresh berries and crème fraîche.

Bruschetta di albicocche, peschenoci, e susine
Apricot, nectarine, and plum bruschetta

For 6

6 apricots

6 very ripe soft nectarines

6 plums

6 1/2-in slices from a sourdough loaf, bottom crust removed (see page 277)

4 ounces (1 stick) unsalted butter, softened

2 vanilla beans

1 1/4 cups superfine sugar

1/4 cup Vecchio Romagna (brandy)

crème fraîche to serve

Preheat the oven to 400° F.

Butter a shallow baking pan. Butter each slice of bread on one side only.

Cut the vanilla beans into small pieces, and pound with the sugar in a mortar. Alternatively, roughly chop the vanilla with the sugar in a food processor.

Halve the fruits and remove the pits. Put the fruits together in a bowl. Stir in the vanilla sugar and the brandy. Leave to marinate for 20 minutes or so.

On each buttered slice of bread break and press two halves of nectarine, cut side down, so that the bread absorbs the juices. Place two halves of apricots and plums, cut side up, on top of each slice, and pour over the remaining juices from the bowl.

Bake the bruschettas in the preheated oven for 25 minutes. They should be crisp on the edges and the fruits cooked. Serve warm with crème fraîche.

Pere al forno con valpolicella
Baked pears with valpolicella

For 6

6 ripe Comice pears
zest (in slices) and juice of 1 lemon
3 tablespoons superfine sugar
1 vanilla bean, split
3/4 cup Valpolicella (red wine)
3 tablespoons brown sugar
Caramel
1/4 cup balsamic vinegar
1 1/2 cups superfine sugar
1/2 cup water

Preheat the oven to 350° F.

Cut a thin slice off the bottom of the pears. Hollow out the core from the bottom. Put a slice of lemon zest, 1/2 tablespoon of sugar, and some of the vanilla seeds inside each pear. Put the pears upright in a baking dish. Sprinkle with lemon juice, cover with foil, and bake for 10 minutes until the juice has been absorbed. Remove the foil.

To make the caramel, heat the sugar and water together gently to melt the sugar, then boil. Remove when very dark, and beginning to smell bitter. Carefully add the Valpolicella. Pour over the pears, and bake for 40 minutes longer, basting every 10 minutes until the pears are slightly shriveled.

Remove from the oven and sprinkle with brown sugar and vinegar. Serve with crème fraîche.

Gelato al ribes nero
Black currant ice cream

For 6 to 8   In London, we would make this with fresh currants in season, but currants are scarce in the U.S. A fine ice cream can be prepared with a jar of currants in syrup, available at grocers who carry Eastern European products.

1 32-ounce jar black currants in syrup, drained
1 1/2 cups superfine sugar
1 tablespoon fresh lemon juice
2 cups heavy cream

In a food processor fitted with the metal blade, purée the drained currants, sugar, and lemon juice. Rub the purée through a fine wire sieve to remove any small seeds.

In a chilled bowl, whip the heavy cream just until it is beginning to thicken. Fold about 1/2 of the cream into the currant purée, then fold it into the remaining cream. Put into an ice cream machine and churn until frozen.

Gelato alle prugne
Plum ice cream

Makes about 1 1/2 quarts

2 cups heavy cream
2/3 cup milk
1 vanilla bean, split lengthwise
5 large egg yolks
2/3 cup plus 1/4 cup superfine sugar
2 pounds ripe plums, such as Santa Rosa, pitted and coarsely chopped

To make the custard, in a medium heavy-bottomed saucepan, slowly heat the cream, milk, and vanilla bean just until bubbles appear around the edges. In a medium bowl, whisk the yolks and 2/3 cup sugar until pale and thick. Slowly whisk in about 1/2 cup of the hot cream mixture, then pour it into the saucepan.

Cook over low heat, stirring constantly with a wooden spoon, until the custard is thick enough to coat the spoon, 3 to 5 minutes. Do not let the custard boil. Strain into a medium bowl and let cool. Remove the vanilla bean halves, scrape the tiny vanilla seeds into the custard, and discard the pods.

In a large saucepan, combine the plums and the remaining 1/4 cup sugar. Cover and cook, stirring occasionally, until the fruit is soft and boiling. Cool. Rub the plums and cooking liquid through a wire sieve or pass through a food mill.

Gradually stir enough of the custard into the plum purée, tasting as you go, until the plum mixture is creamy, but still intensely plum-flavored and very sweet (it won't taste as sweet when frozen because very cold foods dull the sense of taste). You may not use all of the custard. Pour into an ice cream maker and churn until frozen.

Gelato al limone e ricotta
Lemon and ricotta ice cream

For 6 (1 1/2 quarts)

3 3/4 cup heavy cream
1 cup milk
10 large organic egg yolks
1 cup superfine sugar
9 ounces fresh ricotta cheese (about 1 cup)
2 tablespoons lemon zest
1/4 cup lemon juice

Combine the cream and milk in a heavy saucepan, and heat until just below boiling point. Remove from the heat.

Using a hand-held mixer set at high, beat the egg yolks and sugar together until light and fluffy, about 5 to 10 minutes. Mix a little of the warm cream into the eggs, then transfer all of it, including the remaining cream, back to the saucepan. Heat over a very low flame, stirring constantly to prevent curdling. Remove when the mixture is thick, but do not boil. Cool completely, then chill.

Roughly break up the ricotta, but not too much, otherwise the texture of the ice cream will be lost. Add the lemon zest and juice and the ricotta to the cream mixture, and mix briefly. Pour into an ice-cream machine and churn until frozen, or freeze in a suitable container.

Gelato con vin santo
Vin santo ice cream

For 6 (makes about one quart)

Vin Santo is the Tuscan dessert wine made from the grapes that are left to dry from October to January. They are then pressed to make a concentrated yield which is aged in special small oak casks called Caratelli for at least four to five years.

7 organic egg yolks
2/3 cup superfine sugar
1 1/3 cups cream
2/3 cup Vin Santo

In a large, heatproof bowl, whisk the egg yolks, sugar, and Vin Santo. Place over a saucepan of simmering water. The water must not touch the bowl. Cook this custard whisking constantly, until the mixture is hot and triples in volume (185° F on an instant-read thermometer, 3 to 5 minutes). Transfer to another bowl, cover, and cool completely in the refrigerator.

Slightly whip the double cream and stir into the cooled custard. Pour into an ice-cream machine and churn until frozen, or freeze in a suitable container.

Gelato alla nocciola
Hazelnut ice cream

For 10

The intensity of the flavor depends on the careful roasting of the hazelnuts.

1 1/2 cups heavy cream

2 cups milk

5 large organic egg yolks

2/3 cup superfine sugar

Praline

1 cup (5 ounces) hazelnuts

2/3 cup superfine sugar

1/3 cup water

Preheat the oven to 400° F.

Combine the cream and milk in a large heavy saucepan and heat until just below boiling point. Remove from the heat.

Using an electric hand mixer, beat the egg yolks and sugar together until light and fluffy, about 5 to 10 minutes. Mix a little of the warm cream into the egg yolks then transfer the whole lot, including the remaining cream, back to the saucepan. Cook over a very low flame, stirring constantly to prevent curdling, until thick curd. Do not boil. Pour into a bowl, cool, and refrigerate until chilled.

Put the hazelnuts in an 8-inch round cake pan. Bake until skins crack, about 10 minutes. Remove, rub off the skins. Return to the pan, now lightly oiled. Bake, occasionally shaking the pan, until the hazelnuts are well-browned but not burned, 5 to 10 more minutes.

To make the caramel for the praline, dissolve the sugar and water in a saucepan. Boil without stirring (you may swirl the pan though), until almost smoking. Pour over the hazelnuts and let cool until solid.

Break up the praline and blend in the food processor to as fine as possible. Add to the ice cream mixture and stir well.

Put the mixture into an ice-cream machine and churn until frozen.

Peach sorbet

For 6

10 peaches
1 1/2 cups superfine sugar
1/2 cup lemon juice

Blanch the peaches in just enough water to cover. Remove the peaches from the liquid and reserve both. Skin the peaches, then cut into quarters, removing the pits.

Reduce the peach blanching water until you are left with 3/4 cup. Add the sugar and boil to a syrup.

Put the peaches in a food processor and blend to a coarse purée. Mix with the syrup and lemon juice.

Pour into an ice-cream machine and churn until frozen, or freeze in a suitable container.

Lemon granita

For 6

2 1/4 cups water
1/2 cup superfine sugar
1 cup lemon juice
finely grated zest of 1 lemon

In a heavy-bottomed saucepan bring the water and sugar to the boil, and cook until reduced by almost half. Remove from the heat and, when cool, add the lemon juice and lemon zest.

Pour into shallow ice trays or cake pans, and put in the freezer. Allow the liquid to partially freeze, about 20-30 minutes. Mash this with a fork to break up the ice crystals, then return to the freezer and leave for a further 20 minutes. Repeat this process, mashing up the frozen liquid, then returning to the freezer and freezing, until you have a hard, dry, crystalline granita. This takes about 2 1/2 hours. As granita melts quickly, serve immediately.

Granita al caffè
Coffee granita

For 6

4 cups espresso coffee made in an
  espresso machine (use about 9 ounces
  coffee)
1 1/2 cups superfine sugar

Make your espresso by your preferred
method. While hot, dissolve the sugar
in it. Allow to cool. Test for sweetness
and strength, and add a little water if
too strong.

Place the liquid into shallow ice trays or
cake pans, and put in the freezer. Allow
the coffee to partially freeze, about 20-
25 minutes. Mash this with a fork to
break up the ice crystals, then return to
the freezer and leave for a further 20
minutes. Repeat this process, mashing
up the frozen coffee, returning to the
freezer and freezing, until you have a
hard, dry, crystalline granita. Use
immediately. Serve with crème fraîche.

Granita alla melagrana
Pomegranate granita

For 6

15 ripe pomegranates, to make 1 quart
  pomegranate juice
3 lemons
1 1/2 cups superfine sugar
6 tablespoons bitter Campari

Cut the pomegranates in half and
squeeze as for oranges. Strain out the
seeds and pith. Squeeze the lemons in
the same way. Stir the sugar into the
lemon juice, then add the pomegranate
juice. Taste for sweetness. Add the
Campari and stir well to make sure the
sugar has completely dissolved.

Pour the liquid into shallow ice trays or
cake pans, and put in the freezer. Allow
the juice to partially freeze, about 20-
30 minutes. Mash this with a fork to
break up the ice crystals, then return to
the freezer and leave for a further 20
minutes. Repeat this process, mashing
up the frozen juice, returning to the
freezer and freezing, until you have a
hard, dry, crystalline granita. This takes
up to 2 1/2 hours. Serve with crème
fraîche.

Tartufi de cioccolato amaro
Bitter chocolate truffles

Makes about 3 dozen

2/3 cup heavy cream
14 ounces bittersweet chocolate, preferably a strong, extra-bittersweet variety,
   very finely chopped
4 tablespoons unsalted butter, softened
Dutch-process unsweetened cocoa powder

In a large saucepan, bring the cream to a boil over medium heat. Stirring often, cook the cream until reduced to about 3 tablespoons. Remove from the heat and add the chocolate and butter. Let stand for a few minutes, then stir until smooth. (If necessary, return to very low heat and stir constantly until melted.) Pour into a large, flat plate. Cover and refrigerate just until set, about 1 hour.

Using a melon baller or teaspoon, scrape across the chocolate so it curls into a tight ball, but do not press the chocolate into a solid sphere. If the chocolate is too warm or too cold, it will not curl. Roll the truffles in the cocoa powder. Refrigerate for at least 30 minutes before serving.

Notes on ingredients

This is not intended to be a comprehensive glossary, but to provide information on certain specific ingredients which we use in our cooking. For more information on ingredients, see the glossary in *Rogers Gray Italian Country Cookbook*.

Anchovies The best salted anchovies come from Spain, from the fishing ports of Omdarroa and Zumai on the Bay of Biscay. The season lasts from April to June. The fish are caught, sold, graded, salted, and packed all on the same day. First the anchovies are graded by size, the largest and most perfect being called "Bar 1." These are always packed in 22-pound cans. 35-pounds of fresh anchovies are carefully layered with coarse sea salt in and on top of the cans, using a collar, then pressed with cement blocks over a period of three months until they fit into the can. Anchovies graded "bar 2" are salted and packed in the same way in 22-pound and 11-pound cans. Anchovies graded "bar 3" and "bar 4" are the smaller fish. They are selected, salted, and packed into large barrels and pressed in the same way for three months, then washed, filleted, and preserved in olive oil. Spanish salted anchovies from 22-pound cans are sold all over Italy, usually by the gram. Stalls selling just salted fish can be found in many markets.
To prepare salted anchovies taken dry from the can, rinse under a slow-running cold tap to wash off any salt and carefully pull each fillet off the bone. Pat dry and use immediately or cover with extra virgin olive oil.

Borlotti and Cannellini Beans **To prepare** dried borlotti and cannellini beans, first soak overnight in a bowl of cold water to which you have added 2 tablespoons of baking soda. **To cook** (for 9 ounces dried beans), first drain the beans, rinse well, and put in a saucepan with 1 large fresh tomato, a handful of fresh sage, and 1/2 bulb of garlic, unpeeled. Cover with cold water, bring to the boil, then reduce the heat and simmer gently for 1-1 1/2 hours. Remove any froth or scum that comes to the surface. When the beans are tender, remove the tomato, sage, and garlic but keep the beans in the cooking water until ready to use.

Brandy Vecchio Romagna "Etichetta Nera" is a rich-flavored Italian brandy made from a blend of wine spirits from Trebbiano di Romagna grapes. It is matured in small oak casks and aged for three years.

Capers Capers are the small flower buds of a shrub that grows wild throughout the Mediterranean. The smallest capers, considered the best, come from the island of Pantelleria. After picking, the buds are dried in the sun then salted.
To prepare salted capers, rinse thoroughly under a running cold tap for 1 minute. Taste to check if they are still salty. Leave to soak in a bowl of cold water for half an hour. Rinse again and use immediately or cover with red wine vinegar.

Chickpeas To skin drained chickpeas after cooking, lay them out on a clean towel, cover, and rub with a circular motion to loosen the skins. Place the rubbed chickpeas in a bowl of cold water – the loose skins should rise to the top. Skim off the skins, drain the chickpeas, and use.

Eggs Organic eggs with a dated laying stamp are the best to use, especially for ice cream. They also carry a stamp showing that they are approved by an organic certifying body. If eggs are not date-stamped, test for freshness by breaking an egg open on a flat plate. The yolk should remain ovoid and the white should be thick, jelly-like, and hold its shape.

Farro This is a type of hard wheat known as "spelt" in English. It has been grown and used in Italy since Roman times and is now mostly grown in Lazio, Umbria, and Abruzzo. A famous wedding soup of these regions is called "Confarrotio."

Honey Raw honey is from bees which have not been fed sugar and which has not been heat-treated or filtered during extraction.

Lentils Castellucio lentils are grown only in Norcia, an arid plain specifically designated by the Italian government as a lentil-growing area. The totally organic production by a farmers' co-operative is obliged to conform to very high standards. Castellucio lentils are available from specialist shops (see page 351).

To cook lentils, put them in a small saucepan, cover with cold water, bring to the boil, then skim. Add 1 clove of garlic and a celery stalk, turn the heat down, and simmer gently for 35 minutes or until the lentils are cooked. Drain and season. Remove and discard the garlic and celery.

Mustard fruits Mostarda di cremona is a piquant preserve traditionally served with Bollito Misto. It is made of candied fruits such as peaches, apricots, pears, figs, and cherries, which are preserved in a honey, white wine, and mustard syrup.

Olive oil The kind of extra virgin olive oil we use for cooking is different from the estate-bottled oils we use for pouring over bruschetta and adding to soups. The cooking oil is a blend of several extra virgin olive oils from all over Italy, produced from olives that are pressed when they are fully ripe and have dropped from the trees. Ripe olives produce more oil when pressed and have a higher acidity. The resulting oil has little flavor or aroma but is much cheaper and is fine for general cooking.

Estate-bottled cold-pressed extra virgin olive oils have very distinctive characteristics and flavors. We go to Italy every November to coincide with the olive harvest and choose oils to use in the restaurant in the coming year. Tuscan oils, which are thick, green, and fruity, have always been our favorite. We choose two that complement each other from different estates and our current extra virgin olive oils are from Selvapiana and Felsina.

The oil from the Selvapiana estate is pressed from the "Frantoio" variety. The olive trees grow alongside the famous vineyards in the cooler Chianti Ruffina zone northeast of Florence. The olives are picked early, when green, and pressed in a modern cold press, producing the greenest and most intensely spicy oil. The new oil is bottled immediately and arrives in the restaurant by December, where our customers enjoy Bruschetta al'olio nuovo – a joy that excites us all.

At the Felsina estate in Castelnuovo Baradenga, on the southernmost borders of Chianti Classico, the olives are pressed in the old traditional way. The estate's mill at Farnetella has been run by the same man for the last 45 years. A manual process results in 4 gallons of oil from 220 pounds of olives. The olives are the "Corriegiolo" variety, the greenest of all olives. They are hand-picked and crushed the same day, producing an incredibly fresh, green smooth oil that we have chosen for its long life, low acidity, and subtle pepperiness. We use this oil for salads and blanched vegetables throughout the year.

Salt Sea salt is pure flaky crystals free from all additives, a completely natural product with a better flavor than table salt and rich in natural minerals. Because of its intense flavor, you use less.

Natural coarse sea salt comes mostly from Spain and France. The grains are slightly smaller than young peas and contain desirable trace elements and minerals. The salt is unrefined and is sometimes gray in color. Use this for salting fish, chicken, and pasta water.

Sourdough starter The starter is the essential element in a sourdough loaf. Sourdough is basically flour and water which have fermented at 80° F over 6-10 days, developing the wild yeasts and organisms present in the flour. A sourdough loaf has a distinctive open texture and a strong, slightly tangy taste. It keeps well and is more digestible than many other breads.

As it takes time and patience to develop a starter, we suggest you ask any baker who makes sourdough to sell you a piece of theirs (see also page 351).

Vinegar The estate of Castello di Volpaia at Radda, in Chianti, makes wonderful wine vinegars – "Erbe," with herbs, "Orto," with vegetables, and "Spezie," with spice. We use all three flavors in salads and wood-roasted vegetables. They are available from specialist shops (see page 351).

Index

Suppliers of Italian Foods by Mail Order

Gourmet Italian Grocers

Balducci's Mail Order
P.O. Box 10373
Newark, NJ 07193
800-225-3822

Convito Italiano
1515 Sheridan Road
Wilmette, IL 60091
847-251-3654
Fax: 847-251-0123

Corti Brothers
5810 Folsom Boulevard
P.O. Box 191358
Sacramento, CA 95819
916-736-3800
Fax: 916-736-3807

Dean and DeLuca
560 Broadway
New York, NY 10012
212-431-1691
800-221-7714

Il Cibo di Lidia
243 E. 58th St.
New York, NY 10022
800-480-CIBO
Fax: 212-935-7687

Todaro Brothers
555 Second Avenue
New York, NY 10016
212-679-7766

Vivande PortaVia
2125 Fillmore Street
San Francisco, CA 94115
415-346-4430

Wally's
2107 Westwood Boulevard
Los Angeles, CA 90025
310-475-0606

Williams Sonoma
P.O. Box 7456
San Francisco, CA 94120
800-541-2233
Fax: 415-421-5153

Zingerman's
422 Detroit Street
Ann Arbor, MI 48104
313-663-3400
Fax: 313-769-1235

Specialty Stores

Egg Farm Dairy
2 John Walsh Road
Peekskill, NY 10566
914-734-7343
fresh butter, crème fraîche, mascarpone

D'Artagnan
280 Wilson Ave.
Newark, NJ 07105
800-DARTAGNAN
973-344-0565
game birds, foie gras

Jamison Farm
171 Jamison Lane
Latrobe, PA 15650 9400
800-237-5262
Fax: 412-837-2287
farm-raised lamb

Margie's Naturally Raised Veal
13 Neilson Rd
Nottingham, NH 03290
603-942-5427
farm-raised veal

Murray's Cheese
257 Bleecker Street
New York, NY 10014
212-243-3289
Fax: 212-243-5001
cheeses, imported butters

Phipps Ranch
P.O. Box 349
Pescadero, CA 94060
415-879-0787
hard-to-find beans and grains

Urbani Truffles and Caviar USA
29-24 40th Avenue
Long Island City, NY 11101
718-392-5050
800-281-2330
Fax: 718-392-1704
truffles, dried mushrooms

The authors would like to thank: Chefs **Lucy Boyd, Theo Randall, Darren Simpson,** Samantha Clark, **Celia Harvey, Christine Osmond,** Jamie Oliver, **Alison Manning, Garry Wilson** Editors Denise Bates, Susan Fleming Design **David Eldridge** Photographers Jean Pigozzi, **Martyn Thompson** Extra photographers Ossie Gray, **Tom Kime, Kenneth Gray,** Michael Elkin Touch-ups Jon Summerill Field trips David Gleave **All staff past and present at the River Cafe,** David MacIlwaine, **Richard Rogers**

Library of Congress Cataloging-in-Publication Data   Gray, Rose.   [River Cafe cook book two]   The cafe cook book : Italian recipes from London's River Cafe / Rose Gray and Ruth Rogers.   p.   cm. Originally published: River Cafe cook book two / Rose Gray and Ruth Rogers. London : Ebury Press, 1997. Includes index.   ISBN 0-7679-0213-0   1. Cookery, Italian—Tuscan style. 2. River Cafe (London, England) I. Rogers, Ruth. II. Title.   TX723.2.T86G74 1998   641.5945′5—dc21   97-31864   CIP
98 99 00 01 02   10 9 8 7 6 5 4 3 2 1